Ben Israel

THE ODYSSEY OF A MODERN JEW

Ben Israel

THE ODYSSEY OF A MODERN JEW

by Arthur Katz

with JAMIE BUCKINGHAM

LOGOS INTERNATIONAL • Plainfield, New Jersey

To perplexed seekers who love truth above convenience, especially to my Jewish kinsmen; and to the God of Israel.

"And where are the great and wise men who do not merely talk about the meaning of life and of the world, but really possess it? Human thought cannot conceive any system of final truth that could give the patient what he needs in order to live: that is, faith, hope, love and insight.

"These four achievements of human effort are so many gifts of grace, which are neither to be taught nor learned, neither given nor taken, neither withheld or earned, since they come through experience, which is something *given* and therefore beyond the reach of human caprice. Experiences cannot be made. They happen . . . it is a venture which requires us to commit ourselves with our whole being."

CARL JUNG
The Spiritual Problem of Modern Man

PREFACE

Rare is the man willing to lay open his very soul for public scrutiny, exposing not only his secret acts performed behind closed doors, but revealing his most intimate fears, frustrations, lusts and ambitions. Such a man is Arthur Katz, a "son of Israel."

The naked realism of Katz's search for reality and identity leads him from the Bar Mitzvah to idealistic Marxism to the existential atheism of a "modern man" to the inevitable destination of personal failure and despair. Yet out of this came a confrontation with the stark absolute of Revealed Truth, and a commitment to that Truth which has brought radical changes in the deepest recesses of his being.

Carl Jung, the great Swiss psychiatrist, said, "It is from need and distress that new forms of life take their rise and not from mere wishes or from the requirements of our ideals. . . . All creativeness in the realm of the spirit as well as every psychic advance of man arises from a state of mental suffering." Thus does Art Katz qualify for his place in the sun, as we see this "new form of life" unfolding from the pages of this authentic odyssey. Only some names have been changed —the events are true.

JAMIE BUCKINGHAM
Melbourne, Florida

Ben Israel

THE ODYSSEY OF A MODERN JEW

CHAPTER ONE

DACHAU, GERMANY
1953
Yom Kippur

Corporal Golden went to Kol Nidre last night. I picked up a three-day pass and caught the train to Munich instead. What more appropriate way for a Jew to spend the most solemn day in the Jewish year than wandering through the concentration camp at Dachau, preserved as a kind of grisly memorial?

I was totally unprepared for what greeted me at this museum of death. I walked through the facility—the barracks where those gaunt Jewish skeletons were once herded—the compound streets with the whipping posts still in place and the gallows stark against the colorless sky. I entered the Kommandant's office with its glass exhibition cases containing scraps of letters, striped uniforms, implements of torture, photographs of mounds of hair, mounds of teeth, mounds of bodies being pushed into graves by bulldozers—mute evidence of unspeakable horror.

Then the gas rooms with the jets still in the ceiling. Here my brothers had been herded like cattle into cars. Women and children. Stripped naked. Old men and young boys. They stand beside me now, their skeletal forms giving them the appearance of the walking dead. The doors clang shut. The overhead jets open and hiss. I stand in the middle of this great, empty room listening to a cacophony of screams and prayers ascending and echoing off the bare walls around me. I see the macabre forms writhing in agony on the floor, white flesh stretched taut over gaunt bones, all forms of modesty gone as they face the ultimate reality of death. I see naked women, dazed and unbelieving, holding their bloated babies against drooping, withered breasts . . . little children clutching the skinny legs of mothers and fathers, screaming in unutterable terror . . . the floor awash with vomit, blood and human excrement.

Where was the atoning God on that Yom Kippur? Why was His ear silent to the shrieks and prayers of these helpless, innocent ones who were slaughtered like cattle? My stomach turned sick and my eyes blurred with tears. I wanted to strike out in blind rage. I was numb, numb . . .

Outside were the conveyor belts where the bodies were dispatched to the giant ovens. Here the carcasses were shaved of all hair, wooden mallets were wielded by grim-faced men to smash the teeth from the dead jaws so the gold and silver fillings could be recovered, and then the mutilated bodies were slowly and systematically fed into the flames. The huge smokestacks never ceased their ugly belching—twenty-four hours a day as the ovens were stoked with the House of Israel.

I was unspeakably sickened and overcome by the ghastly evidence of man's subhuman conduct. I reeled away, my mind, my nerves, my heart overcome by what I had seen.

On the train I found a compartment and flung myself upon a seat with a groan of despair. I peered unseeingly at the bustling platform outside my window—soon we would be in Munich, the great cultural center of Germany. Universities, seminaries, opera-houses, art galleries—all the hallmarks of civilization. Yet just a vapor away lay that great factory of extermination. How could the people have lived, going about their jobs and "cultural" activities, pretending that monstrous apparition did not exist?

I was sick, sick, sick . . . my forehead burning as with fever, my stomach aching, my legs weak . . .

The train jerked alive and pulled out of the station. I peered through the glass at the idyllic and beautiful Bavarian country-side whisking by. How could a nation that had produced a Goethe and Schiller, Beethoven and Mozart, Schopenhauer and Kant have reached this indescribable insanity?

Surely, I thought, there is an answer to this enigma of our human condition. I sensed in the German people, in their zest for life, their language and culture, something of the hunger for the deep that coursed through me. Could the horror of Nazism be but an expression of this yearning gone berserk? Manifesting its fury by lashing out at the insipid bourgeois civilization which betrayed it?

Still, the incredible horror of an entire nation feigning unknowingness, allowing such bestial cruelty! The reveries of my youth would never return, for into my soul had been etched the stark picture of a sick and ugly world where listless phantoms would forever inhale the acrid smoke of burnt flesh.

The blanket of night was being slowly drawn over the peaceful countryside. How much human folly had it been witness to? The tread and monster-weight of army-tanks had become as familiar as the tractor, which for centuries to come will unearth corroded and decayed evidences of war. I sighed and averted my eyes from the now gloomy and darkened landscape outside.

Until now I had not been aware of the compartment's other passenger. Slowly my eyes focused on a blond, blue-eyed head perspiring in some concentrated effort. An Aryan! I wanted to spit and run. The thought of sharing a tiny compartment with one of "the Master Race" was more than I could bear.

But as my gaze dropped from his face I saw that he was only a pathetic remnant of a man. Instead of arms, a set of hooks protruded awkwardly from his shirt sleeves and his creaseless trousers gave evidence of artificial legs. He was nothing but a torso and head.

The man was writhing in pain as he tried to adjust one of the artificial legs. The hooks kept slipping as he poked and prodded, trying to straighten that grotesquely bent limb, dangling like a broken puppet.

I sat stiffly, arms folded defiantly across my chest.

Suffer, you blond bastard! I thought. *Whatever pain you feel is nothing compared to what your people inflicted upon mine!*

We sat facing each other. The Aryan and the Jew . . . the persecutor and the persecuted. . . . The German and the GI . . . the uniform of the occupation and the empty sleeves and trouser-legs of the defeated . . . the vanquished and the victor. Had he, years before, been one of the rioting, mindless bands of Hitler youth that broke the windows of little Jewish shops? Had he zealously squeezed the trigger for the Reich and been decorated and idolized as a representative of the Master Race? Had he envisioned his blond counterparts mastering and metering law and order to the world's inferiors—of whom I was one? And what had been his thoughts in that blinding, deafening, horrible moment when the shrapnel dismembered his limbs and left him lying in the muck, feeling his lifeblood spurting from the stumps?

Yes, blond Aryan, you have sowed—now reap!

A wave of nausea swept over me. Only a carcass remained to sustain the organs vital to life. Life! The word was a mockery. At best his was a skeletal existence of humiliation, want and despair.

Suddenly compassion moved me, defying reason, even will, and I found myself standing beside him.

He looked up at my uniform, his brow creased with pain, his eyes cautious at first, then smiling gratefully as I bent over him. He showed me how to adjust his leg and I gripped the false limb with both hands, suppressing an involuntary shudder as I felt it strange and lifeless through the cloth of his trousers. An impulse to yank and twist and hear him scream flashed through my mind, but gently, careful not to inflict any more pain, I slowly turned the wooden projection into the proper position and heard him sigh deeply with relief.

I turned to walk away, but his hook tugged at my sleeve. His voice was strained. "Please—sit and speak with me."

I heard myself answer, "Yes, yes of course," and we both smiled and displayed cigarettes at the same time.

"Please, I insist," he mouthed each English word carefully.

"Oh, no, have one of mine." We looked at each other and laughed, then compromised by accepting each other's offer. I held my pack to his mouth so he could grasp the cigarette with his lips.

We smoked in silence. Then he spoke: "You have been in Germany long, no?"

"About eight months," I answered, and told him where I was stationed.

"What do you think of Deutschland?"

"It is very beautiful," I replied, sensing even as I spoke a love welling up within me for its culture and history, its antiquated formality, its language and spirit, and yes, its tragedy and shame. Even the texture of its soil—all had reached out and captured my soul.

I studied the face opposite me carefully, looking for signs of cruelty and barbarism. There were none. His was merely a man's face. Suddenly the unspeakable pity of it all nearly overwhelmed me. We were two atoms brought together in a moment of time, two humans caught up in an inhuman century.

In that instant the truth dawned: *Katz, except for the accident of birth, the caprice of time and place, you might have been born a German Aryan. It could have been you stoking bodies into the ovens.*

I shuddered and looked long into his blue eyes. "I have been to Dachau," I said quietly.

"Ach!" The cold metal of his hook reached out and touched the back of my hand, trying in a fingerless way to express the inexpressible. His blue eyes scanned my Jewish features. "Der krieg. Der krieg. Never again. Never!"

I saw moisture gathering in his eyes as he stammered, seeking a word.

"My brother!"

The words seemed shaped and formed from forgotten wisps, put together from the fragments of time eternal. In them the whole complex structure of mind and emotion, dark and light, culture and mores broke apart with a thunderclap of simplicity.

My brother.

It was so simple it was staggering. Brothers. Kindred spirits. Probing and pushing, filling the universe with the testimony of our essential oneness—our essential lostness. Yes, entwined in a kind of spiritual intercourse we find ourselves mated in our madness, our agony, our despair, our desire. From the ghettoed asphalt of Brooklyn to the soot-stained grayness of Dachau, we are brothers, kindred spirits drifting through a fog-enshrouded world, searching for the light.

CHAPTER TWO

Fez, Morocco
July 1, 1963

Searching for the light. Thirty-four years old and halfway around the world from home. It's as if that day at Dachau had never been, that indelible day when I knew my life's direction —I would become a teacher, make a new world through the classroom, raise up a new generation, drive away ignorance and by my human effort change the world. I felt all my Jewish zeal, my energies and my passion born for that purpose.

But something went wrong.

And today, I'm sitting here in this crummy sidewalk cafe toying aimlessly with a glass of stale beer and watching the parade of humanity on the sidewalk in front of me. My mind is saturated with thoughts: of Helga and seven years of stormy marriage now smashed to bits between our two stubborn wills; of my students at Inglewood High School at Oakland around whom my whole world orbits, students for whose questions I have no answers; of Mother and her influence on my life; of my own sense of failure and my determination to find reality and identity and meaning out of life in these coming months as I hitchhike across Europe. I will journey to the rootland of my ancestry—to stay until I find meaning. But how can one find reality in a setting such as this?

The street scene before me looks like something out of Arabian nights. Bearded and turbanned vendors, old ragged men astride overloaded burros, little boys hammering on brass, pumping billows or holding taut handfuls of colored threads for their cross-legged masters seem to place me in another century. Yet for this congested humanity it is a workaday world, as much for them as it would be for me to walk into my Humanities class at Inglewood and open the floor for discussion. The twisting, narrow alleys are littered with dung, wetted here and there with the overflow of the tiled fountains and the reds, yellows, and blues of the tanner's dyes.

The whole scene is terribly dank, musty and redolent with age. The crumbling walls and turrets go back to the time of the Crusades, and except for the occasional western dress, the scene seems virtually unchanged.

Strange, how the past is so much a part of the present. Directly across the street from where I sit is a kosher butcher shop which reminds me of the murky old red brick synagogue in Flatbush where I attended Hebrew school and took my Bar Mitzvah. The sights and smells of the Casbah, the hashish-smoking men and the constant whining of the Arabic music stir my memory of other sights and smells of childhood—the smell of chalk, wine and urine in the dingy basement of the ghetto synagogue, the old men with yellow-stained beards and long fingernails poring over the sacred Hebrew volumes. The spittoons on the floors. The traditional skull-capped rabbi. It's all part of the scene of the past.

Here in Northern Africa, as I watch the children playing in the streets or peering timorously from behind the long skirts of veiled Moroccan mothers, I hear the sounds of Jewish boys playing stickball in the Brooklyn ghetto and the voice of my mother from a window high above the street, calling me to come in the house "right this minute!"

I watch the faces that pass in front of me—the young and old, the ragged children (they are everywhere in great numbers), the soft look of the young mother carrying her child. I am but an observer, watching. And yet, at the outset of my journey, a sense of desperate adventure grips me also. Europe. Scandinavia. Finally Israel. There has always been this deep longing to go back to the land of my beginnings, to the cradle of my people. Perhaps in Israel I shall find some answer. My life this afternoon seems to be nothing more than a collection of miscellany, without order or reason.

The sight of a soldier, duffel bag thrown unceremoniously over his shoulder, sweating down the sidewalk toward the bus terminal, cries out to me that life is like a duffel bag, jammed with all the mementos of the past, waiting the day when they shall be shaken from their hiding place to be dealt with one at a time.

My orders to be shipped home from Germany had finally come through. I spent the early part of the morning sorting out my belongings. The barracks were empty and I took my time, marveling at the assortment of odds and ends I had collected during the months overseas. I mulled over each one, debating whether to throw it in the trashcan or the duffel bag. Picture postcards. Crumpled letters. Museum brochures. A cardboard beer coaster. Some pocket-size books. A dehydrated and flattened flower. An unused train ticket. A dated opera schedule. A tin of prophylactics—one missing. A key. A ribbon and some coins. A ping-pong ball. Ticket stubs from theatre and opera performances.

All the paraphernalia and accouterments of poignant and half-forgotten incidents. I chilled and warmed alternately, depending on the memories conjured up. All were dropped in the duffel bag. I wondered if years hence they would still have a magic about them, or would they become just so many meaningless scraps. The last to go in were Helga's letters and pictures. I lacked the courage to riffle through them and placed them under my army gear, to be glanced through when I would have the fortitude to battle ghosts. Little did I know then that one day this German fraulein would be my wife and together we would walk through hell.

I promised myself when I left the ship several days ago that I would not spend the time "reflecting," but would look for meaning in the present circumstances. I sense now that this will be harder in practice than it is in theory.

The bus ride from Tangier to Fez (about two hundred miles for three dollars) was an experience worth recounting. As gross as was the evident poverty in Tangier, rural poverty is ineffably overwhelming. Mud wattle and stick-constructed villages spot the countryside, a type of housing that must predate the pyramids. The bus stops whenever a passenger can be accommodated, and some were in such pitiful rags that I marveled when the fare was forthcoming, out of a dirty, knotted "handkerchief." Once we stopped so the driver and some of the passengers could buy goat meat from a roadside stall. Parts of the animal were hung on nails, the whole swarming with flies. Crude chunks were hacked off and weighed, wrapped in paper and thrust under the seat of the bus rider.

At Meknes I had to change buses for the local job to Fez and was squeezed in between two Arabs. They were surly, swarthy types, looking much like pirates, with rags wrapped around their foreheads, casting hostile looks in my direction to suggest that they'd as soon slash my throat as look at me. I tried my best to look tough and well-traveled, but in truth I never felt so far from home as on that hot, crowded bus.

A few days in Morocco have made some things very apparent to me. What is exotic and colorful to the American tourist is someone else's misery and degradation. I saunter through the narrow streets and alleys, among the open stalls, bazaars and shops, seeming nonchalant, but my senses are overwhelmed at every turn. My fingers twitch to photograph these scenes, but somehow my conscience is disturbed at doing so. The natives reveal an integrity and pride which makes the camera in the hands of a hitchhiking tourist an instrument of exploitation.

Tonight, as last night, this section will be crowded with farm people who come to sell their stunted produce on the streets. A piece of cloth is stretched out on the ground in front of the cross-legged vendor. On it he spreads his paltry wares—directly over the urine, spit-stained, dung-ridden cobblestones. Keeping alive is a full-time activity.

As evening approaches the streets become filled with people promenading. So unaccustomed was I to the sight that I had to inquire whether there was a holiday of some kind. Last night I sampled some native food, oily and poor in quality, and today I feel a bit queazy and have not eaten anything since coffee and a croissant this morning. From where I now sit, beery and euphoric, all life seems reasonable and pleasant. Every man has his calling or purpose down to the most humble water-seller or even beggar. With a twenty-cent beer, one can sit here for hours, converse, or meditate, or simply watch the traffic go by. Or, as I am doing, he can toy with and describe his experiences on paper.

In the youth hostel at Fez I met two Germans in their early twenties, who, shoeless and without possessions save the most elementary gear, have been wandering about Africa for over a year. They survive by occasional work and their wits. They had consciously turned their backs on western society, carrying to the extreme what is to me only an anarchistic propensity.

I scoffed when they said Africa was the last unspoiled continent, thinking then wistfully of the idyllic German hamlets I had visited during my seventeen months' military duty in the early fifties. The thought of Germany always leaves me with a bittersweet pain. Oh Deutschland, Deutschland . . . How strange that these two young men seek elsewhere for beauty and reality. I see in their Fatherland something of the Jewish alter-ego, the "second I." How much of me is at home there. Those first meetings with Helga . . . the village gasthaus . . . the GI scene . . .

Ironically, it was I in that conversation, during which they munched their meager supply of bread, tomatoes and onions, who defended man's obligation to his fellows and concluded by accusing them of a kind of perverted hedonism, finding color and diversion in the poverty and degradation of others, who, God knows, hunger for what we disenchanted affluents disavow. Both claimed they'd found a greater freedom and delight in life, and also gained a sense of self not available to the millions insulated by an affluent society. Both seemed to be thriving, especially the huskier of the two whose massive thighs were the equal of a slight man's waist. The other, a scholar, antiquarian and auctioneer in respectable life, is fond of Henry Miller, George Orwell, Durrell and Herman Hesse, so we immediately established a community of interests. I had read *Steppenwolfe* aboard ship and was enormously impressed.

Another interesting chap at the youth hostel is twenty-year-old Carey Binghamton, the image of the tall, sandy-haired elegant Britisher. Yet he is a Jew and a fervent Zionist to boot. He's hitchhiking across North Africa to Israel via Egypt and Jordan where, if need be, he says he can act the anti-Semite convincingly. He's impressively self-sufficient and taught me some useful things about living on the road. He delights in agitating the Arab hostelers, glorying privately to me, comparing the tough Israeli with the adversaries who surround him. It is hard to believe that he and I and the Moroccan Jews I observed in the synagogue are of the same "tribe." Oh, the diversities and yet the sameness of my peculiar people!

Tomorrow at 6:15 a.m. I catch a bus for Tetouan which still leaves me forty-seven kilometers to hitchhike to the Moroccan port city where I can take a ferry across the Gibraltar straits to Algeciras, Spain. It's ridiculous my not being able to speak French or Spanish, a situation which further emphasizes my role as an observer or outsider—unable to "enter in" to the strange lands through which I wander.

And yet now that I have bought sandals, I can pass for a native. My dark skin, black curly hair and prominent nose are easily construed as Arabic or Moroccan, which is much to my advantage. In fact, I have been stopped for information by other tourists who were startled to find I don't speak French. I have just this minute been offered a newspaper by the newsboy moving among the patrons of the cafe—quite a compliment to the likes of me. I have a new mask—without designing it.

Damn this suit of armor. Here in Oakland at Inglewood High School my mask is crumbling under the frontal attack of my students. This constant scrutiny of one hundred eighty kids a day, picking at my mind, demanding that I be excruciatingly honest with myself. But how can I? I have no answers to their problems . . . and then this moral indifference of theirs . . . their concern with cars and girls rather than philosophy and ethics. But even if I could awaken them, to what could I lead them? My own anguished frustrations?

The shattered fragments of my own life. After seven years of childless marriage . . . Helga in the hospital bed, the electric shock treatments seem only to worsen her condition. Thinking that even her thoughts can be heard . . . that one of the doctors is out to "get her" . . . walking like a zombie . . . expressing in that eerie voice her terror of being killed by some unknown antagonist . . . voicing in a pathetic whimper the anguish of all those years since I first met her in Germany . . . and even before.

Helga, sick, but knowing my sickness too, and probing gleefully into that area where I was most tender—gathering enjoyment from the pain she inflicted upon me.

"You're dedicated to egotism, Art—and as arrogant as a Nazi."

I would feel my chin jutting out as I contested her charge, not realizing until later, after the harsh words had been screamed and the vituperative accusations thrown, that by my actions I was simply attesting to the validity of her allegations.

I've tried venting my frustrations to Saul Goldman, my colleague, yet he doesn't seem to understand. "For God's sake, Art, how in the hell do you get yourself into these situations?"

The numbing sense of despondency . . . that life is mastering us rather than we it. In the microcosm of our own personal striving, frustration and futility do we catch a glimpse of the macrocosmic world failing? Am I responsible for what I am and for what my being has done to others?

Did my actions put Helga in that mental hospital?

"Be practical, Arthur," my mother said. "Go back to Helga. Be a good husband to her. Work hard at your profession. Be proud of your Jewish ancestry—and make me proud of you." It is this last, I sense, which is the key to her life—as it is the key to the lives of all Jewish mothers.

"Sarah, have you heard about my boy, David? He's now chief of staff at the hospital . . ."

"Judith, come over this afternoon and let me tell you about my son, Samuel. He writes that the rabbi commends him publicly for his new promotion . . ."

And I can still hear my own mother on the phone. "Ah, Dorothy, you must come by while Arthur is here. He has just completed his Master's Degree and is now to be the professor at a big high school in California . . ."

Jacques Maritain speaks of Israel as "the core of the world, there to irritate it, exasperate it, move it. Like some foreign substance, like a living yeast . . . it gives the world no quiet and has no quiet itself." How perfectly my mother's travail symbolizes, almost reenacts, the travail of Israel. Orthodox Jews still look for the Messiah. Is she looking for Messianic fulfillment in the success of her son?

Mother's anxious face is ever before me. Those few days with her in New York before my ship sailed increased the strain that has been building up over the years—a strain which I seem to feel much more than she. On top of Helga's emotional breakdown and our separation, mother's shrill hysteria drove me almost to the breaking point.

The image of her life across the years rises as spectres before me, and the spectres become realities.

Her workhorse hours in the sweatshops beyond Washington Square, traveling an hour and a half each way daily in the subway crush to wrest twelve bucks a week from the garment trade. Barney, the plumber, who gave me my first ride in a car and took me to my first restaurant and who got us the old house after my father left. Mother, working like a man, tearing out the filthy tile on the floor and ripping off the shredded wallpaper so we could live in pride among our neighbors. The afternoon on the trolley car when the conductor refused, because of my deceptive height, to believe I was entitled to half fare—and mother's fierce denunciation accompanied by the almost hysterical crying, wheedling and anger until he acquiesced. The proud insistence that her sons receive a "Jewish education," and her teary, sentimental face during Bar Mitzvah. Her constant advice, "Be practical," and the charismatic quality of her personality, her storytelling, the life-adorning magic which so enthralled me until I awoke to the horror that she had come to believe her own fictions, and had willed herself into deception because it was so desperately necessary to believe that our lives are not lived in vain. The pain she'd borne—her impoverished childhood, her disappointing sons, Lenny, the incorrigible "nebbish," her deceased husbands . . .

The spectres continue to haunt my present. At home, the recurring episodes of disappointment, heartbreak, anguish of the soul, curses, oaths, accusations and recriminations—followed by periods of unbroken quiet while table continued to be set, and food prepared for sullen-faced phantoms who masticate in eerie silence.

The continual doing . . . and baking . . . and cooking . . . and cleaning. Then the guests, the loud squeals of laugh-

ter, the intense gossiping and finally the mask of seeming delight disappearing the moment the company is gone. Fantastic, the men and women friends drawn by this charisma—none really more deceived about her concealed barrenness than she herself.

I see her standing at the door, shaking her head as I leave for the ship. She does not even know what I teach and is fearful lest I should jeopardize my good fortune by being "impractical" in taking this leave of absence. It is impossible for her to fathom the passions and hungers that cry from the depths of my soul for satisfaction.

Or is it? Strangely, I sense something of my own idealism—however faded and withered—in her own nature. Suddenly I see that her life too has been a continual groping for an intangible something that lies beyond appearances and things. Will she ever find it?

Will I?

CHAPTER THREE

MADRID, SPAIN
July 16, 1963

Two days of wandering through museums have stirred in me
a terrible gnawing. The sight of color in rich swirls or layers,
the feel of terracotta, marble or bronze overwhelms and excites me. How beautiful is the human form—the sumptuous female nude, the straining muscular male, the children at play.
There is joy and delight and beauty, and I stand there drinking
it in. In my mind's eye I follow the motions of the artist with
the work in progress—a dab here, a stroke there. I peer closely
to discover how an effect was obtained and walk back to observe how beautifully it all blends into the whole.

"I can do that," I say to myself, contemplating how the now
finished work must have evolved layer by layer. If only I could
allow my deepest self to be so expressed! What would come
out? The thought of a huge white canvas, blank and ready for
the brush, fills me with terror and delight. How would I fill it?
What would I say? What deep joy and satisfaction would be
mine in the process? What pride at its completion? I am certain that mine would not be of the drip and slash school, an ab-
straction or geometric puzzle, but brimming with life and
beauty, saying something about joy and pain and the very gristle of existence.

Yesterday at the Prado I felt overwhelmed in a different
sense. Perhaps awed is a better word. Immense rooms filled
with Goya, Velasquez, El Greco, Rubens, Van Dyck and others whose names escape me. Everywhere a song of praise to

the human form, from the voluptuous nudes of Rubens to the anguished, ecstatic bodies of El Greco. Such a cascade of tortuous flesh is overwhelming.

Jesus is the dominant inspiration here. Jesus on the road to Calvary. Jesus crucified. Jesus risen. Jesus ascending into the Heavens. I can't understand the power of this theme. Not until yesterday had I caught the tremendous impact of this single figure, Jesus, on the artist. What have we moderns to match it? Where is a like theme to excite the passion and adoration of the contemporary artist? How could the follies of a mad carpenter and a pagan, gentile religion inspire such an outpouring of praise and beauty? I must be honest and admit that the thought is a disturbing one that has lingered with me through the night.

Except for the museums, Madrid has been disappointing. True, it has broad, tree-lined boulevards and illuminated fountains and plazas; but save for the obvious difference in language and minor customs, it is like any other huge modern metropolis found the world over.

I sit now in an open plaza at Santa Anna, a foot-weary, wandering Jew, pondering the sad realization that my search for new patterns of life is frustrated here. All is bourgeois around me. The same swivel-hipped youth on the prowl, slash-mouthed men accompanied by fawning women. . . .

In Seville, Granada and Toledo, narrow-winding, cobble-streeted, sway-backed towns reeking of antiquity, I still found the old Spain. There I stumbled upon fountained plazas, glimpsed through wrought-iron doorways a vision of tiled, flowered courtyards and patios. Each of these towns has its old Jewish ghetto with such street names as Calle Juderia or Calle Levites. In some, the synagogues are now preserved as historical monuments and offer a peculiar blend of Moorish and Hebraic art. The ghosts of my forebears linger everywhere, or so it seems to my romantic fancy.

How "native" the Spanish Jews must have felt prior to their

final expulsion from Spain in 1492. Certainly the beautiful and lavish El Transisto Synagogue in Toledo was meant to be permanent, and the lovely Barrio Sante Cruz section of Seville must have rung with the laughter of Jewish children.

There is a sense of mystery about the Jewish people—at home in Brooklyn adapting themselves to baseball and hot dogs—at home in Spain serving as Dons in the Spanish court—yet always the exile, always the alien. Who knows but that the room I occupied in Seville once quartered, centuries before, a Jewish man like me, secure in his Spanish "nationality," later to be robbed of home and property, exiled to a life of wandering.

On the trains and in the streets I search the faces of Spaniards for the signs of the cruelty, stupidity and blood-lust that their forebears visited on my people at the time of the Inquisition, when the streets of the ghetto ran with blood. I try to picture the age-old animosity between the "edel" (noble) Jew and his alien, gentile neighbor, but see none of this in the modern Spaniard who makes his way through the plaza.

As I write this, seven fleshy, coarse-featured señoras, grim with lipstick, are seated in front of me on the plaza. Their harsh laughter is an annoyance as I try to record my thoughts. My writing thus far seems like inconsequential trash. It is forced and artless—but force it I must if I am going to penetrate to deeper layers and succeed in chronicling my inner reactions, and, hopefully, discover deeper revelations of who I am and the reality of my life.

Perhaps because Madrid is so like other familiar cities, my hotel room and bed seemed especially strange to me, and I wondered last night what the hell I am doing here so far from home. Where is home anyway? Then, too, the sight of comely señoritas, slim and firm-breasted, draped on the arms of males who seemed oblivious of their graces, excited me to envy. I was hungry for love, for caresses, tastes and smells—not only in the carnal sense, but hungry for the solace and delight—

physical and spiritual—that only a woman affords. My mind and imagination played over the past in a sweet torment, now this one, now that one, until I fell into a fitful sleep. Helga's letter had been waiting for me at Cook's travel agency and added to my agitation. Both sweet and touching, it brought back nostalgic memories of those first meetings in Germany ten years ago.

The German beer, the warmth of the crowded gasthaus and the music made me relax. I leaned against the wall, viewing with a heady giddiness the thickening crowd on the dance floor.

Round after round of beer went down as the American GIs flirted, danced with and cajoled the local frauleins. To me they all seemed one, in a jostling sea of blurred smiles and faces.

I tilted my perspiring head against the wall. An outline began to take on a definite shape across the room as my eyes focused on the misty form of a young girl alone at a table. Grey . . . wispy . . . enigmatic . . . soulful. Her head was bent slightly forward as she toyed aimlessly with the glass in front of her. Not pretty, but her face was strong—yet haunting—as if shadowy forces labored beneath. The lines of her jaw, cheek and nose seemed almost foreboding and hostile, but her mouth was full and warm. The grey eyes were large and seemed to shelter a lifetime of hurt. Her slim neck tapered into a willowy body—formless in the folds of her dress.

I found myself staring. It was as if the whole hectic pace of time had slowed to a halt in this moment. She must have sensed something—her eyes looked up to acknowledge my stare—then with a show of confusion her gaze faltered, only to find mine in a look of hopeful recognition.

I don't know how I got across the room. She assented with a nod when I asked her to dance, as if in automatic obedience to my GI uniform. The surging crowd on the dance floor swallowed us, allowing only the slightest shuffle.

*The leanness of her body was pressed against mine, and I al-
lowed my hand to feel the texture and knot of her fingers, as if
somewhere in their moist crevices were some secret communication. My first words were cautious—exploratory. I wanted to
look into the soul beyond those haunted eyes. When she answered me in careful measured English, I drew a sigh of relief.
At least we could communicate. But the tumult of the gasthaus
was deafening, and further attempts at conversation would certainly strain the filmy bond between us.*

*I had a twelve o'clock pass that night. It was time to leave,
and panic rose in me at the thought of never seeing her again.*

"Can we meet again?" No response.

"I say, will you go out with me?"

"Yes, I suppose so."

*I ignored the almost passive resignation of her answer and
shouted excitedly above the din: "Wednesday then, at this
place! Okay?"*

*She nodded and smiled as I elbowed my way through the
crowd toward the door.*

*Outside, the swirling night fog with its tiny droplets of mois-
ture that clung to my face and hands seemed symbolic of her
personality. The glare of the taxi's headlights and the slurred
shout of the Corporal's instructions, "Step on it buddy, we're
late!" jangled my inner thoughts. Slumped in the back seat, I
suddenly remembered—I didn't even know her name.*

*We talked of many things. Her parents were typical of the
Germanic old-worldliness—stern and unrelenting, die cast in
the patterns of custom and formality. They could not understand her variance from the modes and mores of prewar Germans. But this was postwar, and she was suckled on the bas-
tardized compost of the vanquished. Everywhere were the
effects of the occupation—American slang, informality, chewing gum, loud music, cigarettes and always the "fraternizing."
The young German fraulein with a swaggering GI on her arm*

received free favors, free cigarettes, free beer, access to GI rations and nylon stockings and a certain status in a nation whose prime manhood had been killed.

Love, the word or its implications, was seldom spoken or felt. Compliance was mechanical. Out of ignorance and soddenness came pregnancies beginning at fifteen and subsequent abortions by unskilled butchers in the back rooms of small shops. Then, the tour of duty up, the soldiers returned home, leaving nebulous promises at the foot of the gangplank. A generation of women waited, many carrying their fragmented illusions in their bellies.

Helga's old man wasn't a bad sort, and she said he'd felt a certain queasiness over the treatment of the Jews in the neighborhood as the war-clouds loomed on the horizon; but then, he was just a single individual and vaguely hoped all would turn out for the best.

The war machine had a way of taking all separate personalities and crushing them together until all thoughts were the same. So she had been recruited into the Hitler Youth and enjoyed the athletic activities, which brought about a new oneness and purpose with others her age. Her innocent idealism was subverted for purposes beyond her knowing as she dreamed dreams of a great "new order."

The rumbling sound of artillery, the clank of tanks, and the dull thud of falling bombs signaled the overture to a new era.

In time the bombs came to Stuttgart as well. The whine of sirens became a daily prelude to chopped-up streets and crumbling buildings. Between raids, she and her mother picked mushrooms in vacant lots to supplement the proteinless diet. Then, one horrible afternoon they emerged from the shelter to watch in horror as flames devoured their home—all their earthly belongings. She grew pale, thin, nervous and deathly afraid.

At last—defeat . . . mixed with emotions of relief and grief, loss and bewilderment, shame and guilt as the gaseous residues

of Belsen, Buchenwald, Auschwitz and Dachau were un-
earthed.

Out of the debris of the holocaust this child-woman
emerged. The busted doll skull and strewn stuffing bore mute
witness to a lost childhood; through the pockmarked streets of
dead ends and debris she groped for survival and shelter, feeling the changing of her glands, the swelling of her breasts, as
she became a woman.

Occasionally, where her womanhood could earn a favor, she
gave of herself, unthinkingly and without feeling. It was like
picking mushrooms, a means to survival in a sordid, sick, postwar world. Somewhere in the depths of her nature, flinging itself at the iron bars of its prison, was a sensitive spirit desperately seeking an avenue of escape.

To Helga's parents, I was considered "verboten." They set up
rules of conduct, hours of arrival and departure, reports of time
spent . . . all well-meaning but many years too late. They were
injured by her defiance—and hostile to me.

We had clandestine meetings. Like children at the seashore
we gropingly and lightly touched each other's store of shells
and valuables, cautiously wetting our feet in the surf and leaving behind footprints which would follow us forever.

Our love was a hybrid flower—uniting in time and space
two alien cultures and nationalities, nurtured by accident, innocence and need.

Here in a Madrid Plaza I am surrounded by couples chat-
ting, tittering and laughing. I am struck by their obvious and
open attention to each other. Is love for them something simple and self-evident? Or is it that they do not love at all but
practice a mindless self-deception? My own experience shows
us humans to be a self-flagellating, cruel, pain-inflicting
species. Must love, surely at the center of the universe, be always "another country," and we stumbling aliens doomed
never to find home?

Neither "illicit" interludes nor permanent domesticity appeal to me as a solution. Yet what else is there? Is my insatiable greed for a variety of experiences the expression of a sick nature, or one too healthy in a sick world? Or is it that I have not yet found *the one* all engrossing, all fulfilling love? If I found it, would I then be happy and contented, teaching or delivering milk or whatever? Or is the root of my discontent tied up with the search for a more creative life?

Chester, the jaded bi-sexual writer I met aboard the ship to Gibraltar, claimed that our pursuit of love must always be self-defeating, frustrating and painful—even when we find it. But I wonder. Can it be that pure love and creativity at its source is one? Must we then look beyond ourselves, beyond mere human relationships to find it? Is this the unknown land of true reality, true identity, to which I, a wandering Jew, am being drawn by a growing inner compulsion? Yet I sense that entering this land requires a kind of total commitment of self that I have always considered alien to the sophisticated, detached intellect. A burning of bridges . . . a finality . . . a renouncing of total freedom. But is what I now experience freedom? I feel as if I am bound within my own gross insensibility, to suffer permanently from a hint of things I can sense but will never experience.

"The bus leaves for town in ten minutes, Katz." The voice belonged to Sgt. Bray. I could hear his steps retreating down the steps of the barracks. This was the last day. I'd already been mustered out and was dressed in civies. I sat on the edge of the cold bedsprings in the empty room and lit a cigarette. My hand shook.

Downstairs I could hear Sgt. Bray's voice booming at the new troops. "All right, men. This is straight from Captain Watson. In D Company we wear our fatigue shirts inside the pants. Furthermore, boots will be shined every day. If you men . . ."

I looked at my empty locker. My linenless mattress, folded over, revealed the cold, naked cot springs. Not a wisp or sign to indicate that I had ever been there. I wondered if the earth itself could divest itself of remembrances of human occupation were it swept clean and laid as bare as my locker and bunk. In grief, I had suffocated in shed tears in that pillow. In rage, I had pounded my fist on that locker door. In mirth, I had wrestled and cavorted on that cot. They had all heard my confessions and stood as mute witnesses to my foible and folly. Now all was back in order.

Outside, the crunch of boots against the gravel drive gave sign of a new occupant. I rose and stood at the door, casting one last look down the aisle flanked by metal cots, knowing that when I stepped through the door it would be as if I had never been.

Is it possible that this is to be the tragic commentary written over the names of all but those chosen few who leave their mark on history—that when we die it will be as if we had never been?

CHAPTER FOUR

I spent fourteen exhausting hours in a third-class coach leaving Madrid at 10:00 p.m., arriving here at noon the following day. My fellow passengers spoke not a word of English, but cordially shared their wine, fruit and water. They were obviously curious about me, and made several attempts at conversation, without much success.

One tall, thin fellow, dressed in blue jeans and polo shirt, carried a number thirteen lucky charm in his watch pocket. He was a novice torero on his way to Costa Nova for a vacation. He showed photographs of himself in action and handbills advertising himself on the programs of various third-rate arenas. He indicated by motions that he had numerous scars from bull's horns about his groin.

Later, I watched him as he slept, the mouth of the taut-skinned bony face wide open as he snored with a slight rattle. I thought of the third-rate club fighters in America who are nursing dreams never to be realized—always waiting for the "big time," wasting their lives away in dreary arenas, clutching a fistful of crumpled handbills as their passport to fame.

My first impression of Barcelona was not a happy one. Worn from the long train ride, I took a cab across town to the youth hostel. Through the cab windows I saw a drab, modern city without Madrid's fine boulevards and fountains. At the hostel I had to wait for over an hour for the hosteler to show up. I was disgusted and travel-weary and went by Cook's, hoping for a sign of life from the world I left behind. Thank heavens there was a letter from Saul.

LETTER FROM SAUL GOLDMAN

I've spent a good part of the weekend thinking about you. I appreciate the description of Morocco and Spain. Some of the images flashed in my mind as I drove out MacArthur Boulevard on my way home tonight. I compared them with what I saw—neon lights, pizza parlors, hot dog stands, gas stations. America—a land without a past.

I took Helga for a ride yesterday. We drove all the way out to Walnut Creek and had a hot fudge sundae—try to get one in your part of the world! Helga looks a little better, but is still quite depressed, thin and pale. She seems to think you'll come back to her before the year is out, and of course, she harped on the old question: "Why did he have to go to bed with Rachel?" I tried to soothe her, saying that after all you two were separated when you did it, and of course I tried to hint that your future might not include her at all. She still loves you, Art, and if you don't mind a bit of advice from an old buddy—lay off writing sweet compassionate letters to her. She showed me one where you even remarked that maybe your whole trip is in vain, and you'd be better off back home with her. Now if that's the kind of stuff you're going to write in July, you damn well better write something similar in December, or she may crack up for good. (She keeps thinking of you as one person; I see you as three.) While we're on the subject, I've been wanting to step out of line and make a small comment myself on your running around. Was it necessary to sleep with a woman and then deliberately tell your wife about it? Didn't you know what that would do to any woman's ego? Don't mean to hurt you, but you know I'm rather fond of Helga in a big-brotherly sort of way, and she's really a pathetic creature nowadays.

I reenter Cal in September to work on a Master's in English.

*In the meantime I'm working part-time for Marty doing some
administrative work at the Institute for the Righteous Acts—
the documentation center on the rescue of Jews in the Nazi era.
I handle correspondence with rescuers and rescued, and it is
very interesting—all about how Catholic priests risked their
lives to save Jews, and so forth.*

*I'm going to throw a sentence from your own letter right
back at you: "Despite an exhausting day yesterday, I spent the
night in a strange room tossing and turning—wondering what
the hell I was doing there, depressed at the seeming purposelessness and restlessness."*

*You seem lonely, friend. Your letter to Helga hints at that
too. I hope you can stick it out. In a sense you're making this
journey for both of us.*

*May all the guardian angels defend you, and may the True
God reveal himself to you.*

                                        Existentially yours,
                                        Saul

Oh, the tangled web we weave . . . and perhaps I am the
master-weaver of them all. Rachel . . . Helga . . . why? I remember Helga's horror when I told her. Would I not still have
told, had I known for certain this would be the crushing blow?

Putting half the world between me and the erupted fragments of my past hasn't lessened the pain or confusion—nor
brought a solution. Did I vaguely hope it would all disappear
magically when I could no longer see it?

Last night I met Jerry Mandel, another Jewish soul in
search. Our conversation started when he tried to sell me his
scooter, since he's now going back to the United States. He's
been gone from home for ten months—first hitchhiking across
America, with a stopover to speak to James Meredith. Then he
worked his way to Israel aboard an Israeli ship. He lived in a
kibbutz for a few months, and finally traveled through Italy to
Spain. He is working on a novel, but has none of the "arty"

earmarks one expects from an aspiring novelist. He was delightfully matter-of-fact about everything, professing no earth-shaking theme for his book, which is intended as a chronicle of the effect of college life on two boys. He's a pre-law student at Cal in political science and has his eye realistically set on the rewards of life. I was impressed by his self-sufficiency. His trip has cost him four hundred dollars. His Jewishness seemed incidental, and I listened in vain for any revelation of deeper significance that he might have received in Israel—the land of Abraham, Isaac and Jacob!

This morning he was gone without a word or note.

July 24, 1963

I met Salvador at the youth hostel, a twenty-seven-year-old bearded Gibraltan who is attending a university in Ireland. His giggle seemed a bit strange at first, but in the three days we've spent together, I've come to enjoy his company. His English and Spanish are superb, enabling me to carry on a fascinating two-and-a-half-hour conversation with a Spanish anarchist who was very philosophical and quite high on existentialism. I enjoyed the verbal fencing-match and trust I made an impression on the fellow!

To escape the 11 p.m. hostel curfew, Sal and I took a cheap room in town. Much of the incentive for this came from Sal who saw an opportunity to lose his virginity through the office of my brashness in dealing with prostitutes. He spoke freely of his obsession with the question of sin, which had brought him near to a nervous breakdown and finally led him to leave a seminary where he had been preparing for the priesthood.

We walked the streets of the red-light district in the rain. Never have I seen such a collection of caricatures of womanhood. They were all ugly and artless in the use of makeup, and seemed to have stepped out of the canvases of Toulouse-Lautrec. The swarms of men who congested the narrow streets seemed to be the lowest order of humanity themselves. On every block was a clinic or two selling creams, contraceptives, hygienic devices, etc. Here the men repaired after the dirty business was over. It was one of those rare occasions when the grossest stereotypes prove to be the ultimate truth. Prostitution must surely be the vilest of all occupations, and one can easily imagine the nightly abuse that had made these women the gargoyles they were. Needless to say, Sal and I returned to our room—he still a virgin.

The early morning sun made my eyes hurt as I stepped through the companionway onto the deck of the lumbering Liberty ship. We were at dockside in Cantania, Sicily, and I had just turned seventeen.

To the starboard I could see the bay where a row of half-sunken ships, their bows sticking out of water like tombstones, were silent reminders of the war just ended.

Last night was still very much with me. The two Italian prostitutes had taken over the old gunner's quarters in the stern, and the entire crew had lined up, bantering and joking, taking pictures through the portholes and passing the wine bottles.

Stomach in a knot, I got in line too. It was bad enough to be called "Sammy" by the anti-Semites on board, but to be a virgin was inexcusable. I had thought sex was going to be the key to the kingdom of happiness, but last night was a nightmare of polluted, sweaty, grunting commerce. On shore you can buy a guitar for a pack of cigarettes; for a single cigarette you can buy a thirteen-year-old girl for the night.

My hand tightened on the rail of the fantail. The sun had cleared the horizon and the bows and masts of the sunken ships cast sharp shadows on the water. This was a new day and the foul tastes of yesterday could be forgotten. Casually I glanced down at the mirror-smooth water below. There, rolling gently on the ebb tide amidst the foul scum that washes against the

*wharf, was the stark reminder that our yesterdays are always
with us. The water was covered with limp, discarded, floating
prophylactics.*

COSTA BRAVA, SPAIN
July 26, 1963

Sal and I took a train to Arenys Del Mar on the Costa Brava,
went for a swim, flirted with two German girls and hitchhiked
the following day to another seaside resort loaded with tourists, mostly English.

That night we went to a cabaret devoted exclusively to
young Limeys of the shopgirl and machinist class. Their faces
all lacked the illumination of intelligence, and they danced in
an unimaginative joyless manner which was decidedly not
Spain but England. I watched one good-looking blond boy
slouched against a wall in that universal ill-at-ease noncha-
lance, ogling a waitress and later giving her a one hundred pe-
setas bill for a coke and stupidly bidding her "keep the
change."

This morning we've toured the Roman ruins towering in the
cliffs above the sea. It is a scene to make the senses drunk with
color—red sandstone cliffs, deep-green gnarled cypresses and
the transparently blue rock-strewn sea. I envisioned the scene
as the Romans knew it long before the invasion of tourists and
souvenir-shops, and envied them! This afternoon Sal goes back
to Barcelona and I go on by bus and thumb.

AVIGNON, FRANCE
July 28, 1963

I've spent the entire day wandering through this walled, historic old city with its marvelous castle of the Popes. At the
youth hostel I met two very interesting chaps. One is a twenty-
year-old Portuguese who spent two months in jail as a result of

political student activity in opposition to the Salazar regime. It
is refreshing to meet a radical of his stripe again. He speaks
fervently of the poverty of his people, the domination of the
capitalist class and the suppression of freedom in his country.
He told me of the interrogation he has been through and a
month in solitary confinement in a cell in which he could not
stand or stretch out fully. He never revealed any of the information the authorities sought, and now is on his way back to
Portugal after a tour of France—in all probability to face other
trials. Americans are despised, he says, for their political and
economic support of the fascist regime, and also for their bad
manners as tourists in Portugal.

The other boy is a seventeen-year-old Belgian named Jan,
tall and thin with a tremendous shock of hair which exagger-
ates his exceptionally prominent forehead and large skull. The
features of his face seem crowded into a small area—the whole
impression is one of cerebral brilliance, borne out by his
linguistic ability (Flemish, German, English, French), wide
reading and very able conversation. Jan is critical of Western
Europe, which he feels is over-civilized and narrowly national-
istic. He likes Italy best and describes it as the least civilized
(most honest and direct) of the countries he has visited.

He travels on almost nothing, living on bread and stolen
fruit. I treated him to a meal, took his address and promised to
visit him in Belgium. Again I am struck by the tremendous
self-sufficiency, amounting to audacity, displayed by these European kids. They certainly make their American counterparts
seem a tame lot indeed, and skip from one language to another
with the greatest facility. Their English is even better than that
of most Americans!

I shall hitchhike on from here toward the Swiss border. My
restlessness is very much with me, and the chance meetings
with fellow wanderers seem only to accentuate this feeling of
purposelessness. Those who have traveled for months, even
years, seem no closer to finding any answers than when they

left home. A common denominator for them all seems to be an extremely negative and critical attitude toward their own country. Always the negative is stressed, and I, the cynical wandering Jew, find myself suddenly yearning for a glimpse of goodness. Strange!

CHAPTER FIVE

I arrived here yesterday only to find the youth hostel full. Tired, hungry and sweaty, I was waiting at the bus stop for the bus back to town, wondering where I was going to sleep, when a young man spoke to me in German. He introduced himself and invited me to his home. I gladly assented, and soon found myself seated at a well-decked table with Helmut and his very sweet young wife Anna.

They insisted that I spend the night, and Helmut borrowed a mattress from the landlady, although I would have been grateful for a piece of floor on which to lay my sleeping bag. They even moved the baby's crib to their own room—though it had to be dismantled twice—so I wouldn't be disturbed at night if she awoke to call for her mother.

Helmut and Anna are Germans, but prefer living in Switzerland because they feel it is freer and more democratic. They dislike strident nationalism of any kind and see nothing unusual in asking a penniless foreigner to stay for the night. "It is the Christian way," said Helmut with a smile. The label made me wince, but I must admit I felt completely at ease in their home and presence, and we spent the evening talking over coffee and home-baked cake. I repeatedly asked if I might not pay them for their hospitality, but they would hear nothing of it, only stating again that this was "the Christian way."

Helmut may have understood some of my present sensitivity to the subject of religion. I find my thoughts returning with increasing frequency to the question of the reality and presence of a living God. At any rate I appreciated the fact that he kept the conversation on neutral ground, impressing me the more with his deep, unspoken concern and compassion for my well-being.

Anna is attractive in a large-boned yet softly feminine way. The apartment is cheerful and neat although far from luxurious, and I experienced just a small twinge of envy as I watched Anna care for her husband and daughter efficiently and with obvious joy. I thought of her as the perfect counterpart to Helmut, who is something of the restless dreamer and visionary. I saw between the two of them something tender and beautiful, yet solid. Though they are obviously quite different in temperament and background, they are yet one in a bond of love quite unlike anything I have ever seen or experienced.

How much of my life is lived beyond the articulate realm— in the sphere of feeling and sensing—areas that are impossible to express! The surface of our marriage may have seemed smooth; but beneath the outer dimension was a turbulence, boiling and seething, searching for some crack, some flaw in the exterior through which it could erupt.

There are satisfactions, gratifications and needs which, if denied in the normal course of the day's relationship, seek compensation in the bed. But when one is incapable of love, this aspect of the relationship also becomes sickly, filled with erotic and psychic demands amounting to little more than exercises of mutual masturbation by compulsive egotists, suckling everything to sustain themselves.

Love is not here. How can it be? Our resentments are expressed in long periods of abstinence, broken by violent sexual skirmishes. The bed becomes a battlefield of unspoken animosities, venting all the resentment and bitterness that can well up between two naked egos forced to share a life together without love.

*We are but symbols of our sick society, for in ten thousand
bedrooms silent attitudes are being exuded in gestures, manner-
isms, even bodily rhythms that bespeak animosity, vexation
and acrimony—rankling the very souls of the ones with whom
we are intimate. What should be the very moment of ultimate
tenderness is turned instead into an orgasm of shattering devas-
tation.*

BERN, SWITZERLAND
August 15, 1963

Thumbing my way to Geneva I was picked up by a French-
man named Bernard and his party of tourists. Only one of
them spoke a few words of English, but I had not been in the
car two minutes before they invited me for lunch at their resort hotel. After lunch they took me on to Geneva, although
this was completely out of their way. Furthermore, Bernard insisted that I spend a week at their place in Paris when I pass
through there.

First Helmut and Anna in Locarno last week, now Bernard.
I don't quite know what to make of such generosity and hospitality to a complete stranger. I have no doubt it is genuine—is
there after all an innate goodness in man?

Geneva is a rather elegant and touristy city with a charming
old quarter. Saturday morning I walked through the outdoor
market, where every kind of foodstuff and miscellany is sold,
and drank in the savory smell of bread, sausages, cheeses, veg-
etables and fruits. What abundance—what deep, rich colors
and fine quality of wares!

At Fribourg I found my first "truly" Swiss city. It is off the
tourist track and rich in medieval color. That is also where I
stumbled into a rather unfortunate and disturbing experience.
At a gasthaus late one evening I met Rene, a former actor and
female impersonator who runs a kind of antique and junk-
shop. He invited me to his place after hours for tea and asked

me to stay for a few days. He offered to show me the town and
surroundings and then drive me to Bern. I was pleased and
taken with his hospitality until the following day when he
showed his homosexual colors and declared his "love" for me.
I, in turn, beat a hasty retreat at the first opportune moment.
Perversion it seems, like the quest for love, is universal.

Bern is thoroughly delightful and seems ideally to combine
lovely countryside and river settings with historic sections. The
city has its touches of elegance without being as ostentatious as
Geneva.

At the dormitory I've met two Indian students with whom I
will continue on to Interlaken. It has been raining on and off
for the past week, and we are hoping for clear weather and an
opportunity for some mountain climbing.

INTERLAKEN, SWITZERLAND
August 18, 1963

We arose early to begin our climb and by noon had reached
a plateau on the Grindelwald, eight thousand feet above sea
level.

Neither pen nor palette could possibly convey what I saw—
and felt. The brilliant whiteness of a glacier against the trans-
parent blue of the sky, rugged mountain peaks, with the towering Jungfrau more than five thousand feet above us, waterfalls
cascading toward the deep green valleys below.

My Indian friend climbed onto a huge boulder, where he
sat, legs crossed under him in yoga fashion, eyes on the distant
horizon, with a look of rapture on his darkly handsome features. I could envision a Tibetan monk contemplating the blue
peaks of the Himalayas.

I felt myself light-headed, almost giddy, as if with each deep
draught of cool mountain air into my lungs, my entire being
was washed clear of the cluttered debris of civilization. I felt
my weary brain soothed by the total absence of noise. The soft

sound of the wind between the boulders and swishing through the mountain-grass served only to accentuate the utter silence around us.

Here on a mountain in the Swiss Alps I could sense finite man's longing to transcend the puny limits of his being, to reach beyond himself to oneness with the source of the universe. In a moment of madness I wanted to cry out into the whistling wind: "WHO ART THOU?" I shuddered, however, and turned my face downward toward the valley, as I realized the answer would come only in the form of the same question: "Who art THOU?"

Zurich, Switzerland
August 20, 1963

The pleasure-pain of this day must be recorded, even as I feel the acute sense of loss after seeing Mary off at the station where she caught a train for Paris.

That I have known her for just one day seems incredible— yet her openness and genuine goodness made a total knowing possible in just a few hours.

I arrived in town this morning, and, after depositing my rucksack at the youth hostel, took off immediately for the old section of the city. By the river I saw a slender, dark-haired girl whom I automatically took to be either German or Swiss. She was alone, feeding bread crumbs to the ducks, and laughing at their splashing antics with such joyous abandon that my attention was firmly caught. She turned to find me staring, and I stammered a less than fluent apology for my rudeness in German. Imagine my embarrassment—and delight—when she laughed heartily, extended her hand in greeting and said, in obvious midwestern American, "Hello, stranger. Come feed the ducks with me."

Mary proved to be a Methodist college student from Kansas, a background that would have left me cold had I not been intrigued by her bright smiling eyes, and delightful freedom from self-consciousness.

She told me of her ambition to become a nurse. When I asked her why, she answered, "because we are God's creation and are meant to do good to one another."

The statement sounded obvious in its simplicity, coming from her, and I could not resist asking how she knew she was God's creation, indeed how she knew there was a God.

She stood leaning her head against the trunk of an old tree where generations of lovers had carved their initials within the crude outline of a heart, and I felt an almost irresistible drawing to the light in her eyes—and the fullness of her mouth.

"God is love," she said simply. "I know He is, He lives in me." Against such logic, who could argue?

We walked the narrow streets together, rummaged through open-air bookstalls and sidewalk art exhibits, bought bread, cheese and a bottle of light wine which we shared, sitting in the soft grass near the river, holding hands and laughing as I cannot remember having laughed since I was very, very young.

I kissed her then, finding her mouth as good and full as I had dared to hope. The desire I felt shooting up within me was not tinged with the familiar lust, and we drew apart, both sensing a warmth and a oneness that did not require the stimulant of physical touch to remain.

We spoke of love and she called it something that man can counterfeit, but until he has experienced the love that flows from God he knows nothing about the genuine article.

She munched on cheese and bread and with a hint of seriousness in the sparkle of her eyes said, "One should not sleep casually with a man, because the unique beauty of that experience should be reserved for the one with whom one shares a lifetime."

In sudden anguish I stared across the small space which separated us physically. I saw the abyss of violated innocence across which I could never hope to leap into such an unspoiled, fresh future.

Accustomed as I am to a free, and sometimes casual, use of words in describing women, I found myself at a curious loss, seeking for the right expression of my feelings for Mary. Walking through the darkening streets toward the railway depot, I felt a growing despair at the soon-to-come parting, dreading to relinquish the feel of the slight pressure of her hand in mine.

There seemed to be only one word in my vocabulary, not soiled by overuse, adequate to describe her. Tracing the fine line of her cheek and fullness of her lips with my fingertip, I said it almost timidly: "You are good." It is a word I rarely use, and the sudden flow of moisture to her eyes told me that she understood.

"Not I," she said quietly. "Any goodness you see is a reflection of God in me." She squeezed my hand and turned away quickly, soon to be lost in the crowd at the platform gate.

I was left to my own thoughts, pondering, as I walked through empty streets, the uselessness of our rhetoric and polemics about God, good and evil, and life itself. Truth lies in direct experience, if we are healthy enough and open enough to perceive it. Again my heart is under scrutiny as I ask myself, "Am I?"

It's summer and the job at Pratt and Woolman's isn't bad for a fifteen-year-old kid. At least it gives me a chance to read on the subway to and from work, and sometimes at work, too. Thomas Wolfe, Schopenhauer, H. G. Wells . . . I want to suck the marrow from the bones of these authors, trying to find out what life's all about. Today I heard one of the salesmen talking behind the jewelry counter about Van Gogh and Picasso. My mind whirled. There is so much yet to learn. I must immerse myself in all experience before it has slipped by.

Yesterday I stood at the window talking with Olivia, the left-wing girl who works beside me, filing little gold things and catching the dust in a small pan. Below was the subway entrance near Fifth Avenue. From our ninth floor vantage point we could see the crowds pouring out of that black hole in the ground, streaming down the sidewalks and disappearing into the building entrances. Life's energy, I thought, spilled out on the concrete sidewalks only to be dumped at the close of the day and sucked down those dark tubes like coffee grounds swirling down the drain of a sink. What's it all about? Why are all those people down there? What are they doing? And here am I, making these silly baubles that people wear. For what purpose? Is there a purpose?

A copy of Carl Jung's *The Spiritual Problem of Modern Man* was conspicuously displayed in a local bookstore window, and I picked it up, to find myself completely enthralled with Jung's approach. Here is a concept of the search for spiritual reality that is not an insult to the sophisticated intellect of modern man, but rather an exciting challenge to his powers of reason.

"The truly religious person has this attitude. He knows that God has brought all sorts of strange and inconceivable things to pass, and seeks in the most curious ways to enter a man's heart. He therefore senses in everything the unseen presence of the divine will . . . The acceptance of one's self is the essence of the moral problem and the epitome of a whole outlook on life.

" . . . That I feed the hungry, that I forgive an insult, that I love my enemy in the name of Christ—all these are undoubtedly great virtues. What I do unto the least of my brethren that I do unto Christ. But what if I should discover that the least amongst them all, the poorest of the beggars, the most impudent of all the offenders, the very enemy himself—that these are within me and that I stand in need of the alms of my own kindness—that I am the enemy who must be loved—what then?

"Modern man wishes to find out for himself how things are. And though this desire opens bar and bolt to the most dangerous possibilities, we cannot help seeing it as a courageous enterprise and giving it some measure of sympathy. It is no reckless adventure but an effort inspired by deep spiritual distress to bring meaning once more into life on the basis of fresh and unprejudiced experience.

"In what may be a daring misadventure, one must have no fixed ideas as to what is right—otherwise one takes something from the richness of the experience . . . if something which seems to be an error shows itself to be more effective than a truth, then I must follow up the error, for in it lies power and life."

> —Carl Jung
> *The Spiritual Problem
> of Modern Man*

The bittersweet memory of Mary in Zurich has haunted me since we said goodbye. Yet it isn't the loss of Mary, but a growing sense of a void in me, a distress that goes deeper than the mere confusion of my present life. Is it that I am not seeking just the absence of pain, the soothing of guilt, the stilling of turbulent waters, but something beyond?

This morning provided another encounter I will not soon forget. I had been given a lift for a short distance in a pickup truck by a young washing-machine mechanic. He dropped me on the main road to Schaffhausen, and I stood for a short time watching the cars go by—my rucksack by the roadside—a silent appeal to the passing motorists.

Before long a late model, expensive-looking car stopped just a few feet beyond me. The driver, well-dressed and in his thirties, came around to where I stood and greeted me with a broad grin and a firm handshake.

"Guten morgen! Where can I take you?" he asked eagerly,

and I had the strange impression that he was delighted to see me.

"Schaffhausen," I said, curious about his enthusiasm.

"Good, that's just where I'm going!" My self-appointed chauffeur picked up my dust-covered rucksack and tossed it onto the fine upholstery in the back seat of his car, beckoned for me to get into the front seat and bounced around to the driver's side as if we were old friends off for an adventure.

I had never in all my hitchhiking experience been picked up in a manner quite like this. His name was Edwin and for the first few miles of our journey we talked lightly about the advantages of traveling on foot or by thumb—being able to make unscheduled stops or side trips, meeting all manner of people, really seeing the countries in the raw, so to speak.

I felt completely at ease in Edwin's company and counted myself fortunate to have caught his attention at the roadside. He told me about himself and his background in an easygoing, almost casual way that still left me with the impression that here was a man who knew himself to be the master of his destiny. I found myself glancing at him sideways, as if to "spy him out," wondering what that something was which made him so confident and relaxed at the same time. He had a way of throwing back his head and laughing out a hearty laughter that was compellingly contagious.

Edwin told me he is married but childless, that he has studied voice and art. He is obviously well-read, a man after my own heart! I told him of my teaching career in California and my general disenchantment with our super-materialistic society, which I thought was on a downward spiraling course toward disintegration and decay. Edwin nodded thoughtfully without commenting.

"As a Jew I am particularly cognizant of the double standards of our Western civilization . . ." I went no further. Edwin slapped his right hand against the steering wheel and exclaimed: "You're Jewish! How marvelous! Then you must know that the answer to humanity's present dilemma was revealed to the Jewish nation thousands of years ago!"

Edwin beamed and although I could not quite see what point he intended to make, I could not help but marvel. Never had anyone reacted with such enthusiasm to the revelation of my Jewishness. He acted as though I were something special, some stone plucked from the mud alongside the road only to be discovered, upon rubbing, to be a diamond!

We were coming into Schaffhausen, and Edwin remarked that this town was accidentally bombed by the Americans during the war. *How utterly meaningless and destructive are our endless wars,* I thought. *Where have they brought us?*

Edwin offered to show me something of the town, and we stopped first for coffee at a modest gasthaus. Over the steaming mugs of dark brew he looked up at me with such obvious, sincere interest that I had a sudden urge to pour out my heart to this new friend.

As if he could read my thoughts, he asked, "Tell me, why are you traveling?"

Clumsily, and at the risk of sounding quite ridiculous, I began a sort of stream-of-consciousness confession of a modern man whose life is crumbling and tottering on its foundation. A man who is desperately seeking for a deeper meaning and ultimate truth on which to stand. Edwin took it all in with a quiet smile, looking at me steadily all the time. I poured out intimate details of my Jewish childhood, of Helga, the problems at Inglewood, watching his face for the reaction of impatient disgust that my friends had displayed upon hearing my rhetoric. Edwin's eyes never lost their deep look of compassion. He only nodded slightly, as if already familiar with the details of my life. I felt a sudden and peculiar tightening of my throat and hastily gulped down several swallows of coffee.

Never had I shared such intimate thoughts with anyone, not even Saul. A wave of embarrassment at this obvious display of weakness swept over me, and I looked up furtively to find Edwin's eyes searching mine.

Edwin spoke of the need for a spirit of humility, and said what the world needs is for men to wash one another's feet. As he spoke, I had a vision of the fat, the smug, the contented—humbling themselves to wash the feet of the lowly and despised. It was as if a light had flashed on in my mind. *How much deeper*, I thought, *is this simple spirit than any philosophy or ideology of which I'd ever heard. Overnight, bloodlessly . . . it could change the world! What have contending ideologies brought mankind after all*, I reflected for the first time, *but contention, strife, suffering and death?* I was suddenly caught up with the simple wisdom of this strange man and listened intently as he spoke on concerning his philosophy of life.

"This is the way out, you know, Art," he said quietly. "Your prophets of old exhorted their people to humble themselves before God, to 'turn from their wicked ways and seek God's face.' God, in turn, promised to make their crooked paths straight . . ."

"The prophets!" I snorted, interrupting what I sensed was going to be some kind of sermon. "Life is too complex for such naive answers."

"Not just the prophets, Art," Edwin smiled patiently. "Carl Jung, who, incidentally, was born in Schaffhausen—has observed that a personal relationship with God is essential for modern man's sanity."

My intellectual curiosity was aroused by the reference to Jung's amazing statement. How strange that I had just purchased his book! I could hardly dispute Jung's authority on the question of modern man's sanity—only his conclusion that God was the answer.

Edwin leaned forward, put his elbows on the table and spoke almost urgently.

"St. Paul called it 'the foolishness of the cross,' " he said. "Don't ask me why God chose to do it that way. It's simply the necessity for all men to receive Christ, from whom even most Christians have wandered."

He hesitated for a moment, and I had a sensation of tottering on the brink of an abyss so dark and deep that I could never hope to save myself if I fell. "Is it not sufficient for a man to live a Christian life without personally accepting this Christ as well?" I asked.

"The two are one," he answered directly. "The secret is Christ crucified for our sins. Christ risen. A living presence within every believer."

"Preposterous!" I shook my head. "Atrocities have been inflicted on my people in that name." We disputed, yet I could not ignore his deep conviction nor could I close my eyes to his manner and attitude which bore out everything he said.

Edwin insisted on taking me by Jung's birthplace overlooking the waterfall, continuing to talk of the necessity for men to transcend forms and experience God directly. As a final gesture of friendship he took me through the fortress designed by Albrecht Dürer and extracted from me a promise to visit him upon my return through Switzerland. He said he would be happy to procure a job for me if I should wish to stay for a while.

We parted the best of friends. There must be *some* reason behind Edwin's serenity of mind, a serenity for which I so desperately yearn. Will I ever find it?

It has rained on and off all day, and I wandered through the streets waiting for the afternoon river-boat while the conversation with Edwin continued to run through my mind. The paradox of the obviously well-schooled intellectual basing his philosophy of life on the fantastic claims of a mad carpenter from Galilee is a haunting one.

I picked up Jung's book and devoured it in a couple of hours. I am greatly relieved that Jung speaks of the necessity of man's search for and experience with God the Creator and

Ultimate Source of all existence, without limiting that experience to the Christ I find myself so loath to consider.

Yet never have I met a man so fully alive—so whole—as Edwin.

And the memory of Mary under the old tree in the park flashed through my mind. She had said, "I know He is. He lives in me."

FREIBURG, GERMANY
August 27, 1963

On the river-boat from Schaffhausen to Stein-am-Rhein I struck up a conversation with a German couple whom I had noticed soon after we left the dock. They were quite distinguished looking, and I caught them glancing at me repeatedly. Shortly before we reached my destination, they came across the deck to introduce themselves. He was Hans Maier, a painter and teacher of art near Stuttgart. They invited me to join them at Richenau Island in the Bodensee where they were staying. "It is a beautiful, historic spot. It would be a shame for you to pass so close by without seeing it," he said.

Later that evening, after wandering about Stein-am-Rhein like a lonely dog, and hiking up to the Gothic castle through damp and eerie woods, I decided to seek their company at the earliest possible moment.

Hans met me at the dock, having procured a room for me at the fisherman's cottage where he and his wife were staying. His wife prepared a snack of cheese and wine, and we whiled away the hours with relaxed conversation about books and art. I was delighted to find how close our sympathies and interests were.

An artist friend of Hans' joined us for a time and shared with exuberance his dream of penetrating to the essence of life with his paintings. I felt that evening as if the four of us were part of a larger fraternity of "outsiders" transcending any question of nationality. How much more we were united in mutual sympathies and a common world outlook than the nationalities which divide us. I went to bed that night, warm and happy, and slept better than I had in weeks.

The next morning Hans took me to a crumbling eighth century church where we spent an hour sitting on the back pew, surrounded by peeling frescoes, while he reminisced about the Germany of the 1930's and 40's. He told of growing up in a village near Ulm, and that he had not even met a Jew until he was a young man. He demonstrated a keen understanding of the political and economic aspects of Hitler's rise to power, but I was far more intrigued as he poured out his heartbreak and vicarious guilt over the injustices his people had inflicted on the Jews. It was as if he found relief in confessing this to me, and he told me how he had known and greatly admired an elderly, well-to-do Jew in Vienna who was an expert on horses. One day in the late 1930's, Hans went to visit him and learned that he had abruptly disappeared. How incredible it had seemed that such things were taking place in his fatherland— yet he was powerless to change it. He delayed his military service as long as he could, and avoided combat, detesting nationalism and the notion that one must serve one's country, right or wrong. He loved his country and felt the period to be totally tragic and the generation that caused it unwitting. Still, he was not sure that enough wisdom had been derived from that experience that it could not happen again.

How completely I identified with him as he must have felt then—caught in a situation not of his own making, impotent to change it or even resist. He had been dragged into a war of which he disapproved and forced to become an enemy of those he so greatly admired—the Jews. Toward the end of the war he had found faith in Christ and with it, he said, strength to endure.

"How is it that you Jews have been unable to see in Jesus Christ your true Messiah?" he asked me.

It was a question I had not expected to hear from this sensitive understanding friend of the Jews, and I rapidly listed some of the more obvious answers—the persecutions, the oppressions—all in the name of Christ.

Hans' eyes held a look of acceptance, not reproach, and he offered no argument in return. I was grateful. I have begun to feel myself haunted by the ghost of that Galilean, since I have accidentally stumbled onto a succession of his followers.

Hans and his wife, with their little dachshund, walked me to the boat that afternoon in the pouring rain. I insisted vainly that they remain in the shelter of the house, but they accompanied me down the hill to the dock. As the boat left, they stood on the pier, poor Hans bravely holding aloft a small umbrella which was quite ineffective against the driving rain. How symbolic of his whole life—the valiant effort to withstand the deluging forces about him. Despite our differences, I sensed we were brothers and pilgrims in this alien world. I felt a deep regret and sadness at seeing them fade from view as the steamer pulled out into the Swiss lake.

CHAPTER SIX

STUTTGART, GERMANY
September 1, 1963

It is as if I have taken a giant step backward in my life. I walk familiar streets encountering ghosts of the past whose shadowy forms inflict the pain of bittersweet remembrances. Today I have retraced the old path from the army post to the house where Helga once lived.

I ran the last two blocks, slowing my pace to avoid appearing conspicuous as I approached the apartment building. The key was warm and leaden in my hand. I turned the lock slowly and let myself in. The silence of the hallway was deadening and ominous. I climbed the stairs in darkness, not wanting to risk the use of lights at that late hour. The floor creaked loudly beneath my foot, and I muttered a soft curse under my breath.

Finally her door. The familiar opaque glass welcomed me in the darkness. I listened and could hear only my own loud heartbeat. That gentle fear tugged at my gut again. Ever since the time I found the unfamiliar cigarette butts in the ashtray— what if another man was there now—with her? I winced and assured myself, "No, it cannot be."

The key scraped and finally found its place. The lock turned and jarred, the tumblers sounding like great weights crashing and falling. I closed the door silently behind me and strained my eye for her in the darkness. Enough pale membraned light filtered through the single small window to dimly illuminate the gentle rising and falling of her sleeping.

I sat on the edge of the bed, leaned over and kissed the sleep-fragrant cheek. She sighed and turned toward me in her drugged drowsiness and put a hand to my face.

"Beautiful angel," I whispered, "it's me. Diene Katzle."

She groaned and wakened, throwing an arm around my neck. "Oh Katzle, you've come!"

The joy in her tone compensated for all the pains and risks I had taken in getting there. "Let me see the face of my Arthurle," she said, snapping on the small bed lamp. "It's better than all the medicine in the world."

My eyes adjusted to the light and focused on her sallow face, pale and drawn. "What did the doctor say?"

"Oh nothing, Katzle, it's really not anything."

"Really not," I mimicked.

She smiled. "It's my kidneys again, and my back hurts. That's all."

"Well, what did the doctor say?"

"At first he thought it was kronisch, but he changed his mind."

"Do you mean 'chronic'?" I wished I knew about this stuff. I felt helpless and ignorant.

"All I have to do is wear my unterhosen and long woolen stockings," she added. "It is just an infection or something. But let's not talk of it, Katzle. I feel better already now you are here. Come, rub my back."

I felt the sleekness of her body through her nightclothes as my hands massaged her fragile frame. Here, I thought, was my fortress and my strength. In her, and in my love for her, I could meet and conquer anything the world could ever throw at me. I was the victor of victors, the god of gods . . .

"How I love thee," my voice was raspy and choking. I bent low over her shoulder and felt myself melting into oneness with her. Our combined weights sank into the wispy vapor and I sought for her mouth . . .

Esslingen, Germany
September 4, 1963

Oh, the memories of this beautiful place! My hand shakes at the very thought of trying to capture with ink and paper some of the thoughts and memories that have flowed so freely since my arrival.

It was here, ten years ago, that I wandered through narrow alleyways and cobblestone streets, sensing a strange familiarity and almost mystical attachment, although I had never been here before in my life.

There was something about this hamlet—something beyond my mental comprehension—that reached out and grasped my heart. Never had I felt such a strong affinity—almost a spiritual relationship—with any place. Could it be what Jung calls "the strands of ancestral consciousness," these strange recognitions that are transmitted from generation to generation?

It wasn't until I returned to the States and began work on my master's degree at Berkeley that I ran across a reference to Esslingen in a history book. There it told how rampaging Crusaders compelled the entire Jewish population of this medieval city to lock themselves in the synagogue where they were burned alive! All in the name of Christ!

CHAPTER SEVEN

Cologne, Germany
September 9, 1963

On my way to Cologne I stopped in Butzbach to look up
Theodor, my black German friend.

The ten years since we last saw each other have not been
kind to Theodor physically! He has lost some hair and gained
weight. But he still makes a most impressive appearance, was
delighted to see me and introduced me to his lovely wife and
beautiful children. He told me he has gone back to the university and now holds a position of considerable importance with
the State Department in the area of African affairs.

Before driving to Cologne, he first drove by the old army
campsite, now deserted and silent. We walked across the
empty field overgrown with weeds and shrubs and I could hear
the voices of the past echo in my ears.

*It's a soggy, cheerless Saturday afternoon and the grey mist
permeates the cracks and flaps of our GI tent, plunging us all
into an aura of sweet melancholy. We've spent the week in the
hills outside Butzbach constructing the rifle range, and wel-
come a respite from the drudgery of digging and hammering.*

*Most of us are gathered in a knot in a corner of the tent. The
conversation spins around home, girls, the lousy army, and
"What I wouldn't give if I —" The timeless, aimless talk of
youth, repetitious and full of bloated braggadocio.*

*As the afternoon wears on, someone begins to strum a guitar,
singing in a soft southern voice. A banjo and harmonica join in,*

and suddenly, from nowhere, appear the cognac, beer and bottle of whiskey that went mysteriously undetected during morning inspection. The music flows like syrup—the hillbilly ballad with an endless variety of themes, the sentimental pop tune, the ageless folk song, Negro spiritual, and finally, because we know nothing else, a hymn, sung with wet eyes and beery lips.

We are all comrades together, as east meets west, and the bleached face of the tenement dweller blends with the red freckles and yokel voice of the farm boy from Arkansas.

A messenger stands at the door: "Hey, Katz, some nigger out heah lookin' fer yew."

I broke from the group of GIs, who turned in idle curiosity to see what was going on. The messenger wore a smirk, and I suppressed an urge to knock him flat.

"Don't you guys ever learn?" I lamented instead. "How can you call a gentleman by that name?"

"Naw," the fellow slurred. "He's still a nigger to me."

It was Theodor. I'd met him at the rifle range where he'd wandered down from his little rural cottage to watch the construction. I had been instantly impressed by this black man who spoke flawless German and English and was utterly European in gesture and manner. A refined and cultured intellectual, he was the son of an African prince who had been brought to Germany during their expansionist period before World War I. Theodor had seemed also to enjoy our too brief conversation and had promised to visit me at the army post.

Theodor has put me up in his office-studio in Cologne, where I've just awakened from a refreshing nap. This is a thoroughly charming room with a quiet, productive atmosphere. A large desk and high winged chair stand before the window, which covers almost the entire length of the wall toward the street and floods the room with natural light. On the sill stands a hammered copper kettle holding a large plant. A small table in the center of the room is flanked by two comfortable chairs.

Closets take up the right side of the room, and on the left are low cabinets heaped with a variety of books and prints. A large, solid-looking couch bed is in one corner, and books line the walls. In a small cabinet is enclosed a display of neolithic, Roman, Greek and Middle Age artifacts.

I have browsed through Theodor's rich book collection and am impressed by the wide variety of subjects and authors. Here is Henry Miller, James Baldwin, Herman Hesse and Jean-Paul Sartre, as well as an impressive list of classics—German, English, French and Russian. I also noted a number of books on theology, among them St. Augustine, Pascal and Kierkegaard as well as Bonhoeffer, Buber and Barth. All this reflects the new solidity and stature I sense in Theodor, who seems very much at home and at peace in this "roost."

A man needs such a place where he can retire to read, undisturbed, and work irregular hours without reprimand or interruption from family or associates.

Theodor has two cars and a TV, but is well aware of the dangers of the new affluent life. In fact, I am more impressed with him than ever, and we've had a wonderful time brainstorming a variety of topics. Theodor has the open mind of an explorer, coupled with the ability to "follow through" on any given thought. How exciting to probe together toward the limits of our reason, understanding and knowledge!

Theodor speaks of the necessity of having a fixed point from which to venture out, a place to stand, without which reason is impossible and our lives and thoughts destined for chaos. I can accept the validity of his proposition, but not the fixed point he himself claims to have found—namely Jesus Christ.

I can only trust that a man of his vision and thorough approach to ideas will dare step beyond such a naive and limited view.

September 12, 1963

I met Kasper on the road when he gave me a lift through Schwartzwald to Fribourg, and promised to look him up in Cologne. Kasper is the fastidious bachelor who knows quite a bit about "Yiddishkeit," has many Jewish friends and is an Israel enthusiast, although he's of upper-class Prussian extraction. He looks and acts the affluent American, speaks English well, wears button-down collars and buys his suits in the United States.

Kasper himself seems to be unaware of any need for a deeper life and shrugged off my comments on the spiritual man with a "religion is the opiate of the people" remark. In his opinion we live in a materialistic world where man is in the process of discovering and conquering the secrets of the Universe—even life itself. But he doesn't seem exactly exultant about it.

BERLIN, GERMANY
September 15, 1963

I am trying to recall the mixture of emotional reflections I experienced last night at the concert hall listening to Tchaikovsky's *Pathetique*. The hall itself in its svelte architecture, modern in the extreme, summed up so much of what I felt about the new Berlin, and in a large sense the whole western world. It stands in sharp contrast to the grandiose, bombastic style of the few remaining prewar buildings of Imperial Berlin, and symbolizes the great changes that have occurred in a generation. The old Berlin has been wiped out, and from its ashes has emerged something indefinably new, brisk, energetic and yet faceless. All of the virtues and vices of the contemporary world seem to be present in this bristling city that overflows with handsome consumer goods. Nowhere else have I been so reminded of America.

East Berlin offers yet another reality of a world that still smacks of class struggle and "proletarian truth." Here one has a greater sense of the old imperial city with its Brandenburg Gate, wide boulevards and partially restored buildings. The re-

minder of piles of rubble, empty lots and ruins brings one back
to history and the not too distant past. A marvelous exhibition,
"Germany: 1933–63," traces the rise of Hitlerism and projects
a Marxist interpretation of that period that rings with truth.
So, side by side, separated by barbed-wire and concrete are
two realities that make excellent sense within their own con-
texts. Ideologically and historically I have known the one, and
now, in more recent years, the other, so that the two Berlins
express also large fragments of my own life and help me to perceive better the origins of my own discord. Had it not been for
the devastating Khrushchev revelations about the Stalin period
as well as materials seeping out of Yugoslavia concerning the
recent realities, I might be a Marxist yet, with more than a
sightseer's interest in the affairs of East Berlin.

*"Marx's concept of communism as the ultimate evolution of
all social forms is the only answer to the contradictions inherent in the world's ills." I sat spellbound, listening to the brilliant teaching of Herbert Aptheker, developing a strong, ultimate faith that Marxism was indeed the answer and that the
inner contradictions of capitalism would bring its final defeat
and breakdown.*

*I had railed, since dropping out of high school, against the
status quo, against the deceit and fraud in life, against hypoc-
risy, injustice and oppression with the romantic fury of youth-
ful selfrighteousness. And I saw in Marxism the framework in
which I wished to pattern my own life, shape a new society
and become involved with the first thing I'd ever tasted that
seemed real.*

*Fascinated by their grasp of dialectical materialism, which
gave them a tool for the analysis of social and political situations, I floated, believing that here at the Jefferson School of Social Science I was in the mainstream of all truth.*

At the concert, stirred by Tchaikovsky's romanticism—a
voice of yet another age to which I am heir—I reflected on my

essential loneliness and suspected that only one born in 1929, as I was, could be so without a past and also an alien in the present. This feeling was reinforced by my visit after the concert to the "riverboat" cabaret where a generation of pointed-toe-shoe "twisters" were having at it. It is hard for me to believe that the kind of music and dance that moved me so—and still does—is now largely extinct and that I, too, am "dated."

This visit to Berlin has given credence to Theodor's statement, which continues to ring in my ears, that the world is everywhere the same, Israel notwithstanding. Occasionally I am inclined to accept and make peace with my small portion in life and to do "God's work" in the land I know best, to put my foolishness and "Ubermensch Absichtung," the desire to be a superman, behind me and to fill the voids in my life with painting, music, reading, fishing, playing tennis . . .

But I wonder about my return to teaching, and ask myself, "What have I to offer the kids?" I seem to be a man without a strong viewpoint—with a vision of the world that is full of shadows and insubstantialities. Then, too, can I cure myself of my life-love-zest that is so dangerous—and do I want to be cured? I hunger still for greater meaning and purpose—"greatness"—but am made more and more aware that I have not the stuff of which it is made! There seems to be no niche for which I am pecularily fitted, considering my amalgam of half-qualities, and I have not that intellectual or artistic or emotional power that can lift me to a greater height. Still, I despise mediocrity and the conventional life and yearn for more. I wait for the magic or miracle of love which I need so badly and wonder if it, too, will come in time—or is the fault mine that I have not been able to obtain it with Helga, or with anyone else? I envy Theodor and his beautiful family, but at the same time I am grateful for the independence that is mine. So many questions that "torment" me—questions that require sharp commitment in a world that is ambiguous—are decided for most other men by life itself, so that they have no choice but to follow and make the best of it. It seems to be my lot to chase phantoms, and I pray—if I can use that word—they lead somewhere, in time.

The following passages in Kitto's *The Greeks* excited me very much as I lay across my bed last evening reading.

> *"The tragic turn of thought was habitual with the Greeks. The reason is not that they thought life a poor thing, but conversely because they saw life with such gusto and enthusiasm and delight . . . They had the keenest appetite for activity of all kinds (physical, mental, emotional).*
>
> *"[this] enabled the Greek to see more clearly than some the great framework in which human life must be lived . . . to which even the gods must bow. Actions must have their consequences: ill-judged actions must have uncomfortable results . . .*
>
> *"The tragic note we hear in the* Iliad *and in most Greek literature was produced by the tensions between these two forces. Passionate delight in life and clear apprehension of its unalterable framework . . . Typical of the limitations, even the contradictions of life, is the fact that what is most worth having can often be had only at the peril of life itself."*

In all this I recognize so much of myself that I was nearly intoxicated with the reading of it, and had to fight back the mad urge to run through the halls shouting, "I'm a Greek! I'm a Greek!" Which in truth, I am.

CHAPTER EIGHT

COPENHAGEN, DENMARK
September 26, 1963

Who would have thought, as I entered this strange land of bicycle-pedaling, cigar-smoking demure old ladies, that I would be caught up in experiences that I still can't fathom?

I met Sylvester, an American Negro, in Rendsburg, prior to catching the ferry to Denmark. I was intrigued not only with his strange little two-seater car that runs on a motorcycle engine, but with this highly articulate chap who, like myself, is searching for his identity. He had journeyed throughout Africa, hoping to find something of the roots of his being, but came to the realization that he is too much a product of western culture to be at home in the bush. He comes from a Baptist home, but had pushed that aside as part of the Negro culture he was repudiating. He had great aspirations for Scandinavia, having heard that the people were "color blind" and that he could therefore find a place in the midst of their society and be recognized for what he feels himself truly to be. The fact that Sammy Davis, Jr., American Negro entertainer, had recently taken for himself a blonde Swedish movie actress as a bride, bolstered Syl's ambitions and desires no little bit in this same area.

Both of us are contemporary men, minority men, at the periphery of modern society. Both have struggled to success in our chosen fields after impoverished childhoods, yet we are essentially unhappy, empty and searching for the elusive meaning and reality of life.

We got a room in Copenhagen in a private home and the first night found ourselves at a quaint cabaret, a type of high class wine cellar that specializes in dance music. Toward the close of the evening we found ourselves at a table with several nurses and nurses' aides in the company of a repulsive, drunk American. As an afterthought I asked one of the Danish girls to dance, although I was not necessarily attracted by her physical charms. Her name was Inger, and I found her able to speak only a few words of English. We made a date for the next day, and she invited me to Naerum to her apartment.

I want always to recall my sitting bolt upright in bed listening with interest to God, it seemed, speaking through the mouth of Inger. It was a lesson in love, or rather about love and its meaning. In her pitifully inadequate English, she made me see the difference between erotic love, the brand I had long exulted in, and "true," that is, selfless, love. I had been the recipient of her love for the past few days and never had I known such affection, devotion, joy and care to come from one person. She actually delighted in scrubbing my back in the shower! She struck me as that rare person who experiences life directly, who has neither the wit nor sophistication to erect screens between her feelings and her experiences. She knew I did not love her and probably never would, but she loved me, nevertheless, without condition and without stint.

Our last night together I know to be one of the profound experiences of my life. I felt as if I were seeing something of the very essence of love (Is God love?) in the character of this remarkable and simple girl. I asked her what she would do if she had to choose between having me always about or losing me so that I could find myself elsewhere. Without hesitation she chose the latter.

STOCKHOLM, SWEDEN
October 4, 1963

Syl and I are quartered at the youth hostel, which is a floating ship tied at the pier. The first night here we met Britt at
the opera. She was seated in front of us, and we conversed during the intermission. Later she agreed to let me see her the
next day. She is a devout Mormon and speaks beautiful English. I sense in her the kind of girl that would make an ideal
wife. Her long red hair, falling across her lightly freckled forehead, framing her green eyes and full, red lips, excites me. We
have spoken much about God, but I am far more taken with
her personally than with her beliefs. I went along to her
church, and she chided me for engaging in an argument with
two Americans, Mormon missionaries, after the service. She
laughingly pointed out that I look very stubborn when I let my
chin jut out during an argument. Despite our friendly disagree-
ments over religion, I feel a growing relationship—akin to
love—permeating my being, drawing me closer to her and
causing me to dread the day when I must leave her. I keep
wondering if at last I have found a woman, perhaps "the"
woman, who can fulfill my deepest longing. Yet I begin to
sense that my life is no longer mine to give.

OSLO, NORWAY
October 8, 1963 (12:45 p.m.)

Sigrid! Strange girl. The fact that she is Norwegian and only
nineteen is absolutely irrelevant. There is an eerie and timeless—and priceless—quality about her, not only in the expression of her mind and feelings but in her very physical appearance—even the texture of her flesh. I marveled at first that a
girl coming from a small coastal village could understand
Kafka, but not any longer. She has an all-knowing quality
about her—something beyond what we usually call insight—a
knowledge of the deepest recesses of human mystery and mis-

ery. A kind of madness rages in her, simmering beneath a deceptively tranquil exterior ready to burst. She said she would like to meet me in combat, hoping I could master her, and I believe it. Yet I sensed that were I to be intimate with her it would bring about her total destruction.

She has the soul and torment of an Edward Munch, and my wishing her happiness, success or fulfillment was absolutely absurd, for her personality is created for unhappiness. As we talked, I saw in her much of myself, particularly that egocentric disposition that tends to make me view the world as if it were ordered for my edification and pleasure. She stands in the sharpest contrast to Britt who is the epitome of the healthy and whole person, a kind of "mother earth," built for love and children, whose every word almost, resounds with moderation and good sense. There are no dark passages in her being as in Sigrid, yet both are made to create—the one in life and the other in art. One would offer me peace, comfort, beauty and serenity—and the other agitation, discord, even violence. My nature cries out for both.

I curse myself for being too stupid to see clearly what the experiences with these three very different Scandinavian women mean. Each is getting at something vital in my life—each very instructive, particularly in juxtaposition with one another. Is my love so broad that it could reach out and encompass all three of them? Or is it that my untamed nature simply cries out for fulfillment in love, and as opposite poles attract, sees that part of me in Inger, Britt and Sigrid which yearns for fulfillment and leaps forth, hungrily seeking to be united with itself, seeking to be made whole?

I should not close here without some word of Oslo, which reminds me of the United States in the 1930's, and impresses me in obvious and strange ways. The art of Vigeland and Munch touched me deeply, and everywhere here—at the opera and ballet too—the theme of men and women, man and woman together, is constantly being reiterated. I am amazed at the many sculptures, which seem out of proportion to Norway's small population and lesser wealth than her Scandinavian neighbors. There is something primitive and savage that reverberates from the Vikings to the art of Vigeland and Munch and even in Sigrid. Perhaps this proximity to a crude and inhospitable nature does a lot to explain Norway, where on this grey, foggy morning I can't think of a better place for a man to be melancholy or for his mind to be dismembered entirely. I think of Munch's inscription on an etching entitled "Gerchrei," "the scream," to the effect that he screams through nature.

Tomorrow we leave for Copenhagen after an overnight stay at Gotenburg. I find myself looking forward to my next meeting with that strange child of Denmark, Inger.

CHAPTER NINE

I am sitting at the table in Inger's room while downstairs she bustles to prepare a meal for me. Syl and I drove through the night and arrived here at 3:00 a.m. after catching a late ferry across Oresund to Denmark, then pushing on from Gotenburg where there was no room to be had. It was a delicious feeling to hurtle through the dark countryside, musing contemplatively to myself as Syl slept alongside me.

I tried to fathom the pattern of my life as my mind flicked various images of a possible future on an imaginary screen: Katz the sculptor, Katz the painter, Katz the student of philosophy and religion, Katz living in New York, Israel, California, Europe . . . All the while I had the sweet comfort of knowing that I was going to one who would receive me with joy at any hour and in any condition.

When I entered her room she was sound asleep with her two lamps burning, my picture on the table near her, my recent postcard under her pillow alongside the dictionaries. I was startled at first by her apparent homeliness and had to adjust myself to her strange face. But it was wonderful to be beside her, selfishly, where I moaned and cried like a child.

This morning she told me of her pregnancy and spoke of the baby who is to come. I was stunned—especially when I considered the seven barren years with Helga. I tried to convey to her that I am both happy and sad over it. She asks only that I be here in May or June when it will be born. I have promised

that much. Inger herself does not understand how instantly her
heart went out to me, and how she wrestled with her soul
about sleeping with me that first night until she was finally
overcome. She feels there is some purpose and meaning in it all
but counsels me not to plumb for it. She is very happy about
this child, though she admits to some fear about the censure of
others and the prospect of bringing it up alone. She will not
marry me if I do not love her, nor does she expect or want
from me financial support—only that I give her moral support
through the period of birth and explain to the doctor that she
is not an "un-moralesk" girl.

I cannot shake a constant self-interrogation: "What have I
done?" It's incredulous that I have precipitated something I
am not able to correct. My acts, as Kitto says, must have their
consequences. And I am responsible for what I do. How could
I have been so blind to this before?

There is a sense of irrationality in it all. Seven years with
Helga—and no children. Now this homely little wisp of a girl,
for whom I have no feelings whatsoever, has conceived on our
first night together. It was just a lark, and now, BANG, she's
going to have a baby—give birth to another human life—a life
that is, by all that's right and moral, my responsibility, my
child.

What is this life? It all seems so capricious. Through sheer
ludicrousness I have stumbled into something—and now great
consequences are going to ensue.

Strange that I should just this day finish reading Goethe's
Faust. It has left me somewhat perplexed. The theme is the
tragic price that is paid for the ego-strivings of one man and its
expression in the seduction of a girl, Gretchen. Like Inger she
was simple and uncultivated, a girl whose untutored nature
had been won over by the charm and attraction of a sophisticated worldly man. But I do not feel that *our* situation is in any
way tragic, but have a hopeful anticipation that everything is
tending toward some crystallization although every outward

circumstance points toward utter destruction and chaos. Unlike Faust, however, I can still hope for my redemption since my bargain with evil has so far not been irrevocable. (I trust!)

I pray that this fractured life will somehow form into a whole, and often I am nearly overcome when I try to encompass it all. Yet I wait now for the flow of a new experience and direction. In everything God shouts at me as if to say, "How much more must I do for this man to see?" Yet I am still too stupid to see, but feel in time I will see. I want more than anything to do the "good" and "right," and though I am tending toward it, I as yet do not know what it is. I know only that my Mary, Britt, Sigrid and Inger have helped me toward it. God help me to be the good man!

I've promised to write Inger's doctor a letter of explanation. Such a little thing, but I want to ease any embarrassment the poor girl may have to face after I am gone.

October 14, 1963

Dear Dr. Christiansen:

Inger has asked me to write you.

This dear simple girl loves me without qualification, and gave herself to me only after much wrestling with her soul. If there was fault, it was mine—but what man can be blamed for not spurning so great a gift?

I intend to do all in my power for Inger and the life that is being created. Although I have the highest regard, respect and affection for her, I do not love her—and proud and unselfishly loving as she is, she will therefore not marry me. Nor does she want financial help from me, which in any case could not be much since I am cut off from my income while wandering about Europe. She will, however, accept a trust fund for the child, which I shall establish upon my return to the United States. I have promised her also, barring any eventuality that I cannot anticipate, that I will return to Denmark in about May or June to help see her through the birth of the child.

Please do not hesitate to contact me for whatever reason. In appreciation for your skill and kindness shown to Inger, I am most sincerely,

A.K.

· I found this quote from Jean-Paul Sartre, which I had scribbled in my notebook before I left the United States:

"The past does not determine the future. Rather one must say: If you want to have such a past, act in such a way. I can choose and continue a tradition, repudiate or fulfill an engagement, learn from my experience or ignore it, overcome approved weakness or avoid and exploit it; and in such ways I act freely on my past and convert it into motives by my choice in the future."

I am finding that my views have indeed changed, if only subtly, since I started on my journey. The past is indeed an irrevocable part of our present and our future. Our only freedom is in choosing *how* it is to determine our future, not *if* it will determine it.

ANTWERP, BELGIUM
October 22, 1963

After catching a ferry from Denmark to Germany, I was picked up after dark by a young American girl driving a new Mercedes-Benz. She was lonely, hungry to talk and not at all sure where she was going. I persuaded her to go to Amsterdam, via Bremen, where I was relieved for the separate quarters for the night at the youth hostel. I paid for her kindness, however, by having to be in her deadly, antiseptic company for two days.

She was adrift and without direction, intimidated and unable to enjoy the European opportunities. She came along to the Anne Frank house in Bremen, which is now a museum. I suppose I should not have been surprised by her total unresponsiveness, while I, caught up in the pathos of the little attic room where that Jewish family had hidden away from the Nazis, was left unspeakably sad.

I made Antwerp in a day and stayed two days with Jan, the eighteen-year-old intellectual I met in Avignon. We have spoken much about the question of God, in which I now have a deeper personal interest than when we tentatively approached that subject in Avignon. I mentioned to Jan that I now am beginning to feel the pangs of conscience about the failure of my marriage. (A letter from Helga indicated the divorce papers are being processed.) He took me to see his priest, who did not provide the revelation I was hoping for. The priest spoke only of the necessity to do one's duty—and answered point-blank that I should not have left Helga. "In discharging one's domestic obligations to one's wife one pleases God," he asserted. He also spoke of "What God hath joined together let not man put asunder."

Christmas Eve 1953 and Helga was waiting at the Bahn Cafe, pretty and demure in blouse and skirt with her little suitcase at her feet. Her face was pensive, looking inward. She didn't notice my approach.

"Guten abend, fraulein Maekle," I quipped in my broken German.

"Oh, Arthur, it's you!" She smiled in relief and reached for my hand. "How beautiful you look in civies."

We consulted the train schedule and decided to travel that night rather than wait till morning. We would be exhausted when we arrived, but the night has its mysteries and we thought it would be good adventure.

I had made many inquiries and finally decided upon a town

*in Bavaria called Mittenwald. I wanted it to be serene—rural;
I would be satisfied with nothing else. We vowed not to mention my coming departure for the States; nothing would mar
the joy of these three days together.*

*The first few hours on the train were energetic and spirited.
We played games—she enjoyed them, but I felt my patience
strained when she framed her clues illogically. Suddenly a dark
premonition came upon me, and I thought how little I knew of
what lay beneath the moody exterior of this child-woman of
the century. I shook it off, and we took alternate dozes on each
other's shoulders, smoked, chatted and dozed again.*

*Munich. We got off the train and patrolled the deserted
sleeping streets at 4:00 a.m. We almost forgot the time, as we
walked by shop windows, peering in through the darkness to
see what hidden secrets we could find. We had to run for our
train, and breathlessly seated ourselves and watched the city
slip by in a cloud of steam, mixed with silver streaks of the
coming dawn.*

*The train was local and stopped at every little country ham-
let. We pressed our faces to the window of the almost deserted
coach and drank in the Bavarian countryside.*

*The sun was straining to crown the new day. Its pale glow
haloed Helga's head and filled me with a new vision of her
ethereal loveliness. The ominous thoughts of the night before
were gone, and I clutched her hand to keep her ever near me.
Turning from the window, she looked into my face and kissed
me without speaking. I wanted her more than I had ever
wanted her before.*

*The longing had grown from a fledgling impulse to an obses-
sive passion with the passing hours. Each time I had been with
her had its own uniqueness and intensity—a brand new experience made richer by her lovely familiarity.*

*We had made no reservations or arrangements. Rather, we
preferred the surprises of spontaneity. We stopped at a small
shop to buy a woolen cap for her and a scarf for myself. The*

*snow crunched delicately beneath our feet, and the warmth of
the little shop felt good. After our purchase, the woman at the
counter shyly inquired if I weren't Jewish. When I confirmed
her impression she sadly related her love affair with a young
Jewish student before the war. One night he'd been taken
away, to become a victim of the incinerators, without even a
chance to say goodby. She patted our hands as we left, expressing her deep nostalgia at seeing a Jewish boy and German
girl together on the streets of Mittenwald.*

*We found lodging with a chatty and solicitous Hausfrau
near the edge of town. The house itself attracted us—a stucco
neo-Bavarian structure with a rustic balcony facing the Alps. It
had all the elements of romance and warmth, framed by the
snowy Christmas-card landscape.*

*The landlady showed us to a room with a balcony, and left
to prepare the immense breakfast we had ordered. We were
tired and ravenously hungry. We washed and freshened, our
familiarity having grown to the stage where we no longer felt
the need for false modesty. Joining in the center of the room we
stood for a final look at each other before going down to breakfast.*

*Outside our window I saw the majestic scene of the snow-
covered Alps rising into the misty morning sky. Helga slipped
behind me and encircled my waist with her arms, her head buried between my shoulder blades. The warmth poured from her
softness against my back, and the whole burden of desire that
I had carried through the night battered at my senses. I whirled
to hold her and found her trembling. Breakfast was forgotten . . .*

BRUSSELS, BELGIUM
October 23, 1963

I've spent almost a whole day in bed in my YMCA room,
reading, reflecting, sleeping and dreaming. More and more the

idea of becoming an artist grows appealing. I envision a monu-
mental cycle of works, magnificently conceived, designed and
colored, depicting those universal moments in which the vision
of God is revealed to men—moments when they are utterly
pierced through by an experience common to all yet timeless
and eternal. My mind has dwelled upon concept after concept,
but the one that persists—I have tried to capture it on my
newly purchased sketch-pad—shows a man cupped in the
arms of his beloved. His eyes are open, looking away from her
as if trying to understand the glimpse of eternity he has just experienced. Her eyes are closed as she strokes his hair, her smile
reflecting deep joy and satisfaction. I realize how easily such
themes become overly sentimental, but perhaps it is my peculiar mission to give man insight into God and life through such
art. I realize that such an ambition and the necessary skill to
attain it might absorb the balance of my lifetime. Oh how I
long to say something, something unique to my own makeup
and experience! Perhaps this is it.

I toy in my mind with various concepts of God, and yesterday wandered into two churches here in Brussels, hoping
somehow to sense His presence. I found myself muttering,
"God, this is not Your house." Today I've tried a kind of
prayer-meditation theme that has brought some comfort. I'll
spend one extra day here in Brussels, staying tonight at a Fran-
ciscan monastery thanks to Jan's arrangements so that I can
see *La Boheme* tomorrow night and attend a university dance.
Then off to Brugge, Oostende and London.

October 24, 1963 (6:15 a.m.)

The soft crunch of the monks' sandaled feet against the
gravel of the path beneath my window wakened me at dawn.
Sitting here on the windowsill of my monastery room I can see
them below, heads bowed in meditation, hands clasped piously

in the long folds of their brown robes, walking slowly, silently, around the manicured garden.

The morning air is crisp and scented with cedars. Inside the monastery wall, foliage is vivid with autumn, and the tops of the silver maples catch the sun streaming across the roof of the castle-like building where I am staying. My attention is drawn to the flower garden beneath my window. Peering through the ancient lattice I see that the frost killed the roses. Yesterday they were radiant—this morning they are brown and wilted. Soon snow will cover the garden, and I shudder as if the chilly winds swirling from the north are touching my very soul.

I wonder at the miracle of spring.

October 24, 1963 (midnight)

The music and mood of the opera tonight have stimulated my nostalgia almost to the point of tears. How could Puccini have such a marvelously deep grasp of the heart of man? In the final act Rodolpho tells Mimi she is as beautiful as the dawn. Mimi says the simile is wrong—he should have compared her to the sunset. Then, as if in a dream, she sings the poignant phrase from her Act One aria. The two lovers recall incidents of their happy past, how they fell in love, how they looked for the key that night in the darkened attic room. Rodolpho reminds her that Destiny guided him. But overshadowing the entire scene is a foreboding cloud, as one senses that Rodolpho's tenderness and Mimi's attempted light-heartedness are vain attempts to forestall the tragedy to come.

Tonight with a light autumn rain pelting the ancient windows of the Belgian villa within the monastery walls, caught up in the reverie that still tugs at my heartstrings from the haunting melodies of the opera, I try to recall my own past. Happy moments? There have been so few.

Tomorrow, and tomorrow, and tomorrow,
Creeps in this petty pace from day to day,
To the last syllable of recorded time;
And all our yesterdays have lighted fools
The way to dusty death. Out, out brief candle!
Life's but a walking shadow, a poor player
That struts and frets his hour upon the stage
And then is heard no more; it is a tale
Told by an idiot, full of sound and fury,
Signifying nothing.

Even as Macbeth, lamenting on the death of his love, once glimpsed the guiding hand of "destiny" on his life only to lose it because of his follies, so I, tonight, wonder if my life also is doomed to tragedy.

CHAPTER TEN

I have been in London two days now and am well taken care of by my mother's family. After leaving you, I stayed a few days in Amsterdam, which was very pretty, and then two days each in Antwerp, Brussels, Ghent and Brugge before arriving here. I met a Catholic priest in Brussels and stayed overnight at a monastery where I had the opportunity to discuss the question of God which so interests me now. I feel that I am coming closer to some very important understanding and change that will make me a better person, but it will take still more time. When it comes, it will give me the kind of happiness I have long needed, and perhaps finally end my restlessness.

LONDON
November 6, 1963

I am restless and agitated, disturbed and in pain. Tonight, my last in London, we saw *The Deputy*, which, like *The Possessed* of a few nights back, touched on the question of human depravity and moral responsibility. Uncle Howard's comments at intermission and on the way home in the car were unbearable—he merely dipped down into his businessman's reservoir of appropriate clichés and surface banter and thereby relieved himself of the obligation to think and feel. "That madman Hitler—to think one man could do such damage!"

There was a moving and philosophical final scene in the

play, a confrontation between the Auschwitz SS Doctor and the martyr priest, in which the whole question of God's existence is most brilliantly presented. Of course I cannot help but reflect: "What kind of God is it that permits such evil in the world?" and "In the face of such evil how can there possibly be a God?"

It has been a strain for me to be polite, and I think if I were to remain here longer I would erupt. Uncle Howard and his family exist without spirituality or even reflection on life. Business is the sole subject that excites them, and their pleasures are basically material. Their only acquaintance with the Jewish faith is gastronomic, cooking kosher style but casting aside as irrelevant all other aspects of their Jewishness. They are very decent people, kindly—especially Aunt Naomi—but their highest emotion is sentimentality, and no question is ever given to any of the real conditions of their lives. Underneath Cousin Stuart's seeming adaptation to that life are some disturbing undercurrents of sadism and flight from self that his parents are too simple to perceive. I feel that he will, in time, hide further from himself as he is fitted more and more to their pattern of life. It makes me despair, especially because they are decent and yet so beyond reach.

Helga's curious cablegram—"Write me at once, 80 Sixth St."—disturbed me greatly, and last night I had a bad dream, more complex and rife with symbols than any other I can recall, which ended when a rather short and stoutish woman quietly entered the door of Helga's apartment at the far end of a long hallway in which I was standing. I knew instantly that this woman was intent on Helga's murder, as I remembered the day before—in the dream—sitting in the kitchen or foyer of that apartment with a tall stranger who said jokingly, "A woman was murdered by her cousin in this apartment." And, a moment afterward, the same grim woman entered through the door, looked at us without speaking, turned on her heel and left. My effort to reach the apartment to avert the murder was thwarted by clots of people in the hallway, past whom I had to shove and push to reach the door. Finally, I pushed it open to find the room in complete darkness, with not a sound anywhere. Either the murder had already been committed, or, as I hoped fervently, Helga had hid herself somewhere—beneath a sink, I think. At that moment I sprang awake. I am very anxious about the peculiar telegram, and will not rest easy till I hear from her.

This, together with the play and general consternation about myself and God, brought me to my knees in an attempt at prayer. But, like Claudius, I was only too aware that my clumsy words went up while my thoughts remained below.

I finished Durrell's *Justine* tonight also, which, enigmatic as it is, added to my particular sense of life's mystery and poignancy. The last line reads: "Does not everything depend on our interpretation of the silence around us?"

The last leg of my journey now seems a very long one indeed, and I do not anticipate it with the same freshness and sense of joy that accompanied my earlier travels. I am tired of places and movement and want now to be stationary, to read and contemplate. I miss Helga especially tonight and prayed that God would bless and comfort that tortured, unhappy soul and guide me to do rightly by her.

Though I was on my knees, I could not get away from my central concern for self. I asked God to show me His work for me but all the while I knew it was my gratification that really concerned me.

I have not yet accepted the idea of a real and living God, let alone one who might conceivably enter my life in response to prayer.

I think I must ever be doomed to be the vain bastard. I noticed recently that I am startled and displeased when I catch sight of my image in a mirror; my face, so thick and coarse and far from giving any indication of growing spirituality, seems actually to be changing in the other direction, and at times even looks unintelligent. I know that, ironically, if and when it does change to reflect longed-for changes within, I will not care at all.

In four hours I must be up and off to Paris for God knows what.

CHAPTER ELEVEN

I am waiting now at the Gare de Lyon for the train to Fontainebleau from where I will continue my hitchhiking jaunt into Italy.

I came to France with some apprehension about accepting Bernard's kind offer to put me up. I feared that my present melancholy might strain our relationship for all time. On the contrary, it proved to be a most delightful six days, culminating last night in a grand meal at a lovely Parisian restaurant. I tried to tell them how much this visit has meant to me, and also what our first meeting in Switzerland had done to lift my sick spirit and brighten my jaundiced view of the human family. Their genuine kindness to a total stranger who did not speak their language—a Jew at that—has gone far to awaken my faith. There is an intrinsic goodness about them all, especially Bernard, that does not have its roots in any religious framework. So attached had we become that Bernard's mother cried at our parting, and proclaimed me "sympathique" at first sight. I will always remember Bernard coming down to Place Pigalle after work, tired as he was, so that I wouldn't have to spend an hour waiting for the bus.

Paris itself did not excite me as I expected, partly because I am already travel weary, but I think more so because I am sick of big cities and their crowds of stunted humanity. Everything else in France seems drained to add to the opulence of the capital city, which, I think, is hardly worth it. At the Im-

pressionist Museum I viewed Gaugin and was struck by the
thought that he was born with that eerie palette in his head
and had to search for the place that would release it. I wonder
if the same is true for others.

I picked up Sigrid's letter describing her near mental breakdown—she can't stop thinking—confirming my impression
that she is a tortured spirit. Helga's letter was sarcastic and
once again we are at odds, she having completely missed the
spirit of my last letter, which I thought especially tender, if not
spiritual.

This morning I awoke about 5:00 a.m. though I didn't get to
bed until 1:30 a.m. My head was filled with random thoughts
about the future, but especially about the writing of a novel—I
was composing a droll first chapter in my head—which I
thought would be at worst of the Leon Uris-Eugene Burdick
class, and at best, something very good. A statement perhaps
about universal man—a microcosm in the modern world
searching for meaning. Can I do it?

ROME, ITALY
November 6, 1963

The trip from Paris was miserable: grim drivers staring
straight ahead left me standing in the rain up to three hours at
a time. My only compensation was the certainty of the
stabbing of their conscience, for which I am sure they
hated me.

I was picked up out of Lyons first by an engineer, then a
chemist, and finally a traveling representative who helped me
get a ride with an Italian.

Tonight after reading through my mail from Cook's, I sat
down and wrote Britt in Stockholm.

LETTER TO BRITT

*Is it wise for me to write and keep alive your feelings for me
when it is possible that I may cause you even greater pain than*

I already have? How often did I tell you that I was not good enough for you? Among other things, you deserve someone whose feelings are as deep and clear as your own—not one like myself whose emotions are muddied and shifting. I know that if I were with you, I would feel again exactly as I felt before in Stockholm—but now thoughts and feelings intrude and cloud my affection. Try and realize that I am adrift in the world while you are stationary.

Picture me walking the streets of Rome after having read all my mail at Cook's office, mail from different parts of the world. Each correspondent is a different personality with different concerns, and each lays claim to me in some way. I am the receptacle for all, balancing all in my head at the same time.

I feel bad that because of me you have no interest in other boys and are lonely and miserable—when you deserve so much, and I can promise you nothing. If you decide that it will be wiser to be done with me, I will quite understand and not blame you a bit. The girl in Denmark has no claim on my heart, only my moral responsibility—which does not involve marriage—so you need not be concerned about her as a competitor.

One more word. You say my letter speaks not to a woman I love. It is so cold. And here we come once more to that difference between us we've discussed previously. You assume always the sanguine view of human nature and the world—that if one loves one must be automatically warm, generous, etc., because you are that way. Do you not think, that with a less healthy psyche than your own, one can not only be cold to a person one loves, but even cruel? I know I was irritated when I wrote you that last letter. Could it be that I was irritated with myself? I know that once before, I courted a European girl with a different religion and background from my own, for whom I had the most idealistic hopes. I brought her to America and experienced some painful years. In a sense that relationship is not over yet, perhaps it may never be.

You are a person without doubts—doubting neither me nor

God. You know *because your soul speaks through your pure*
nature, and I don't know *for exactly the opposite reason.* That's
why I have the feeling that all other questions are related to
the question of God, and when I "solve" that, all things will be
made clear. The only thing I can guarantee you is more pain,
and I am not being melodramatic. Again I cannot help but see
the striking parallel with God, who requires our lives, yet seems
to offer only the pain of Martyrdom in return. How much more
I would respect Christians if they were "good" simply out of
genuine love for man and God—even at great cost to themselves—and not because they are hoping for some reward in
"Heaven." I am still looking for a man who would be willing to
die to do the will of God.

I have read your letter over and over again. How wisely you
understand the peril of occasional correspondence that reflects
the feelings of only that moment. So, too, am I trying to make
sense of my whole life in which in different "moments" or
stages I have been shown a different part of myself. But
enough of that.

In my mind's eye I sit at your bedside, place my arms beneath your back and lift you up to drink from your mouth.
Many such kisses from your vexing,

Arthur

Yesterday I made final arrangements for my Egyptian passage. I was able to declare myself a student and therefore qualify for cheaper passage, even though it will be deck passage.
Since I feared that no Jews were being admitted to Egypt, I
was forced to declare myself a Christian, and now have in my
possession a Roman certificate which says, "Arthur Katz at-
tests to me this day that he is a Christian." *Anything* for the
cause!

Ironic that the "cause" I agreed to undertake in Egypt is a
mission for the San Francisco Bay Area Jewish Museum, the
same institution for which Saul Goldman is now doing research

work. They are paying my expenses, and since there is some danger involved, I go to it with mixed feelings.

I had a letter from Betty Friedman reminding me that the object of the mission is to obtain from the remnant of the Jewish community, which has dwindled from a population of several hundred thousand to less than three thousand following the two wars between Israel and Egypt, the ancient religious and art objects that have not already been destroyed or desecrated. She seems to think that if they are not rescued at this time, another war would mean total destruction. Many of these have been handed down from generation to generation and are now stored almost carelessly in basements and closets of the synagogues. There are Torah scrolls, inlaid Torah cases of wood and ivory, scrolls of Esther (Megillah), the Ark Curtains, silver Torah pointers—readers of the Torah will not use their fingers to touch the parchment but use these elaborate silver pointers—silver Torah shields, Menorahs, commentaries written by ancient scribes and rabbis, documents and archives of the Egyptian Jewish community, ancient marriage contracts, Mezuzahs and countless other articles of religious and historic significance.

TARANTO, ITALY
December 2, 1963

On my way from Bari to Brindisi where I will catch my ship across the Ionian Sea, through the canal at Corinth and on to Piraeus, I felt compelled to make this detour to Taranto. It was here, at the age of seventeen, that I first put foot on the European mainland. And as in Germany, my memory has been quickened not only to sights, smells and sounds, but to my attitude, now rapidly changing, that man reigns supreme.

A canopy of stars, brilliantly blinking from their sockets, stretches above me. The only sound is the swishing of the

*water as the bow of the ship glides forward, and the faint
THUMP-THUMP of the huge diesels far below.*

*Lying on the bow plate, feeling the rise and fall of the ship
beneath my belly, scanning the open seas for floating mines, I
know this is the life!*

*Never have I seen such an unmarred dome of heaven. I'm
awestruck with the vastness of the sea. Tomorrow night we
enter the straits of Gibraltar where I'll see the lights of North
Africa slipping by on the starboard and the huge granite tip of
Europe silhouetted against the sky on the port.*

*I cannot comprehend the attitude of the other crew members.
To them this is but another dirty job. None of them seem to
sense or share in the fabulous opportunity here to taste life in
its natural setting. Their only talk is Italy—and women.*

*Last night I worked a watch at the wheel, steering by the
compass, and feeling the pulsebeat of this mighty ship under
my control. It was exhilarating—beneath my fingertips the
power to change the course of machinery, and of men.*

Before leaving Italy I must make mention of my shock and
sadness at the assassination of President Kennedy. All Italy is
in mourning. How uncharted, capricious life seems—without
meaning, subject to impulse and moments of madness. Is there
no order at its center? No master plan? Or are all men, like
myself, floundering, subject always to the whims of other men?

CHAPTER TWELVE

CORINTH, GREECE
December 8, 1963

The steerage aboard the Greek ship was jam-packed with
the wildest assortment of folks, babies, chickens and turkeys
imaginable. Huge wine bottles in wicker baskets, cans of olive
oil, bags of food . . . It was almost impossible to thread one's
way through to the head without stepping on someone or
something. The ship pitched terribly on bad seas that night
and I could just imagine the misery below.

Sid Zimmerman, a Jewish mathematician of upper-middle-
class vintage from New York, shared my common misery as a
deck passenger. He is a writer with no real interest in Judaism,
but he has made an ideal traveling companion and one with
whom I can spar with words. He is the closest thing I have
found to Saul since leaving California. We've planned to spend
the next couple of weeks together, touring Greece.

When I mentioned my increasing interest in God, Sid pro-
duced a small, pocket-sized New Testament distributed by the
New York Bible Society, given him when he boarded ship in
New York. Having never even opened the covers of a New
Testament, I expressed an immediate interest and asked him if
I could borrow it to wile away the long hours. He gladly
agreed.

I spent the rest of that evening slumped on deck, jammed
between two Greeks, with the music and laughter of the tourist class passengers drifting from the porthole above my head,
poring through the pages of that remarkable book. I saw from

the very beginning that it was totally different from any other book I had ever read. Drawn more and more to the figure of Jesus yet not knowing who He was, I began to sense that He represented all that the world so desperately needed.

Oblivious of the wild distractions about me—babies crying, men and women arguing in shrill voices, people stumbling over my feet as I crouched against the bulkhead—I read on, utterly enthralled by the vivid exposition of this man Jesus.

How perfectly I could understand His clash with the religious leaders of the day! I could envision those hot debates as He punched holes in the superficial lives of those pious Pharisees.

My mind flashed back to my encounters with people like Mary, Edwin, Hans, Theodor—all people whose lives were witness to the reality of this Jesus.

Here in these pages I found nothing of the insipid, the weak, the wishy-washy sentimental submissiveness I had come to associate with the figure of Jesus. Instead I found stark realism and drama—and a man who went about confronting rather than compromising.

I found myself identifying and sympathizing with this carpenter who rendered perfectly fantastic claims about being one with God—"He who has seen me has seen the father . . . I have come to fulfill the law"—and seemed always to be able to repudiate those who contested His right or His power.

When I came to the episode of a woman taken in adultery (John 8), my pulse quickened as I lived the drama. Here I found a clear-cut case of dispensing justice. The law said that the woman must be stoned. Yet Jesus had been teaching forgiveness, and earlier in the book had actually said, "God sent not his Son into the world to condemn the world, but that the world through Him might be saved." Jesus was trapped. I sensed the relish of those who stood around Him, having ambushed Him into an unanswerable predicament. What could He say?

I closed the book, not wanting to see my new-found hero destroyed. His manliness. His keenness of mind. His courage. His deep insight into life. His compassion and love for the downtrodden. All was to be demolished, it seemed, by a group of self-righteous religionists who had plotted this scheme to get rid of Him because He was threatening their Pharisaic codes of justice and righteousness. My heart actually palpitated, and sweat oozed from the palms of my hands as I fancied the men surrounding Him, their eyes ablaze with hatred and envy, spittle running from their mouths as they gloated over His quandary.

So symbolic, I thought, of the entire human situation as truth comes to grips with selfishness.

What would I say in Jesus' place? I searched my mind, exhausting my resources of logic and reason and finally conceded there was no answer. Fully expecting the worst, I reopened the book and read on. I found Jesus bending over, poking His finger in the dirt. *How like me,* I thought, *stalling for time.* Then He looked up, His eyes meeting the eyes of His adversaries. I could see their contorted faces against His quiet control. . . . His expression—pure, resolute.

"Let him without sin cast the first stone."

I gasped. A sword had been plunged deep into my being. It was numbing, shocking, yet thrilling because the answer was so utterly perfect. It defied cerebral examination. It cut across every major issue I had ever anguished upon in my life. Truth. Justice. Righteousness. Integrity. I knew that what I had read transcended human knowledge and comprehension. It had to be Divine.

In one instant those words leaped off the page and engraved themselves upon my heart. When the shock waves subsided, I sat dumbfounded, realizing that *I knew* God was—and is. Not a God of our own making. Not a God far away. Not a God who can be contained in the parchments and scrolls of the Ark. Not a God who can be boxed in by institutional religion. But a God who lives.

I am still stunned and repelled by this revelation. I frankly admit as I sit here in this tiny room in ancient Corinth, a city made famous because of this same Gospel of Christ, that I am fearful of the prospect of the living God intruding into my life. Furthermore, I am embarrassed and irritated that I found this revelation in the New Testament, and therefore am stuck with Jesus. I am instinctively afraid that I will have to become a Christian and find myself lumped with other Gentiles and Ku Klux Klanners. Therefore I resist. Yet I know that the impress of this truth will haunt me until I find some way of resolving my Jewishness with this revelation of God in Jesus.

ATHENS, GREECE
December 16, 1963

Alfredo Casanova, Venezuelan surrealist, was on the ship back to Piraeus from Iraklion, Crete. Sid had little patience for him, classifying him as one more of a pathetic type whose number is legion. Alfredo is a drunkard and a "pataphysician" —a school, he says, which is based on the absurdity of life. His mother sends him two hundred dollars a month to keep him away from home, where, I gathered, he instigates scandals. On the ship he rapidly got drunk and became the object of delight for the deck passengers, who relish diversion of any kind. His desire for exhibitionism led him to force his way into the tourist-class lounge, where he attempted a striptease. An earlier attempt had led to his expulsion, after which he loudly declared that he would refuse to entertain these "capitalistic whoremongers," since they had scorned his spontaneous offering.

As a deck passenger on the outside looking in, I was made aware of the sharp class distinctions on all Greek ships, and thought the amusements and dancing of the tourist class very emotional, especially in contrast to my memories of Heraklion.

There Sid and I had been invited to attend a party, and we had thoroughly enjoyed the fresh spontaneity of the folk dances and songs.

Alfredo was more drunk the morning after, so I lost my opportunity to ask him about the apparent contradiction in his depreciating the "capitalistic class" while living off the proceeds. He liked me and was particularly impressed at my "childlike" simplicity when I showed him the Bible I was reading. He told me he had been extremely religious as a boy, and this had led to rigidity and sexual frustrations, or so he thought. He likes little boys, especially the olive skin "cute" variety. For a moment I thought I had a flash of insight into homosexuality as an expression of super-exuberance and love of life that in this world must often go unrequited. At any rate, I couldn't help but like him, and felt concerned for his life and apparent lostness.

On the ship to Crete, Sid and I met John, a Cretan, who invited us to visit his village of Zaros if we should chance that way. We did, and he was a bit surprised, but quickly adjusted and became a fine host. Life in this village, and I suppose most of Greece outside the big cities, is primitive. His father looked much older than his sixty years and had not been to Athens since 1924. The family lives in two rooms over a stucco "kitchen" and barnyard combination. Meat was boiled in the crude fireplace, and the room was a bit smoky. After dinner we returned to the cafe where the men folks congregate to pass the time, drink coffee and wine and twirl their beads. They were concerned about the price of olive oil, which means everything to them, and hoped that the new government would help them. I tried to suggest that they are victims of traditional rural one-crop poverty, requiring solutions more complex than price raises. I failed miserably to communicate my philosophy. They were concerned about the drift of the young men away from the village to the cities and countries like Germany. Who could blame them? They thought factories would help them,

and I felt a sense of impotence at my inability to convince
them that factories don't necessarily bring happiness; but I
could see that rural poverty is not a romantic alternative either. The people are very simple and childlike, generous and
warm and often very good looking—especially the men.

At Knossos I was touched by the kind of civilization the
ruins, frescoes and artifacts suggested. As Henry Miller says, it
seems to be based on joy—no defenses, no fears. It is religious
in the best sense, in that every moment is lived to the fullest.
We met Alexandros in the ruins of Paesto, the same guide who
said to Miller in 1940, "God must have sent you." He told us
Miller still corresponds with him and sends him money and
copies of every book he publishes—which I thought was very
Christian of him.

The Acropolis at Athens is, I think, the first "famous" site
I've viewed without experiencing a disappointment in the actuality. It was easy to see how men could consider themselves
godlike at such a commanding height and with such an awe-
some view. I stood on a ledge overlooking the panorama of
Greek countryside and imagined myself to be Zeus, Apollo,
Dionysius, or Pluto. Is it that the breath of God lies dormant in
every soul? Why else would my spirit soar and my pulse
quicken at the thoughts of beauty and power? I allowed myself
to dream of sitting at the footstool of the Creator of all this. "I
will lift up mine eyes unto the hills . . . He watching over Israel neither slumbers nor sleeps."

There must be a God who cares, who understands, who
loves. He must be more than prime mover, Creator, the Force
behind the universe. He must be personal, and if He is, then
surely He wants to reveal Himself to His creation. But how?
How is it possible for the God of the Universe to reveal Himself to the likes of us who prefer to spend our time dallying
with the material and superficial things of life? Is it a mad
question asked by a mad man? Or is it the most real question

I've ever asked? And can the answer really lie in this Jesus? Imagine me contemplating this thought!

I rest my elbows on the rail of the troop-transport and peer out at the horizon. The sea is vast, unbroken. Only water and sky, and occasionally another vainglorious vessel steaming on the horizon, thumbing its nose at the elements.

It is dusk, and the whole horizon is dyed and tinged with orange and gold as I stand on the rolling deck, soaking in the fading sunset. How damned insignificant we're made to feel, *I think. The bigness of all of it made me feel like a speck, a grain of inconsequential nothingness, until I thought of man's ingenuity and skill in building this ship, his courage and intelligence in piloting these seas. Were they the testimony to man's real significance? And the sunset merely a natural phenomenon caused by the sun filtering through the atmosphere?*

Yes, *I think.* Man is the important thing in this world. Everything else, including God, is a product of man's ingenuity or man's imagination.

I take a deep breath and feel the sea on my face. Were I an ape in the forest I would beat on my chest. But I am a bit up the ladder of civilization for that, so instead, I pat the rail of the ship, satisfied with my own importance in the universe, and go below to join my fellow soldiers.

The Greek merchants seem to operate on the theory that any price is the right price as long as they can get away with it. In Athens tonight it was interesting to study the face of the proprietor at the tavern when he calculated our bill and suffered a momentary conflict between greed and integrity. Greed won.

On the trip to Crete I finished reading the small Bible, which raised some perplexing questions. Most perplexing were the concepts of the Old Testament God—vengeful and jealous—compared with Jesus—full of love and kindness. I left

many passages underlined which I hope to have explained in
the course of my travels. Tomorrow we are off for Delphi,
Thebes, Epidaurus and other ancient towns. Next week I shall
leave Sid and sail for Alexandria, and shortly after, I hope, for
Israel.

LETTER TO SAUL GOLDMAN
OLYMPIA, GREECE
December 21, 1963 (1:00 a.m.)

*I awoke a few minutes ago for no earthly reason, cupped my
hands under my head, gazed at the ceiling of the darkened
room and thought of you. At Delphi and now here, in the great
hush of ancient Greece, one would expect untroubled sleep.
But for the past three nights mine has been broken and agitated—for reasons which I can only describe as "occult." My
mind goes back now to the image of a great flock of ravens cir-
cling endlessly over the ruins of Delphi, as if working out the
terms of a fated sentence, the spirits of men doomed by the
gods to watch from above while troops of callow tourists pick
their way about the site of their former glory, leaving crumpled
cigarette packages and chewing gum wrappers in their wake.*

*Well, dear chap, the next thing is how to bridge the events of
these many months, or not so much events as interior changes
which are far more difficult to describe. I have a feeling that I
may disgust you when I write that the most important change
centers on the questions of God and faith, which I do not ever
recall our discussing as it was simply not relevant. I am taking
only tentative first steps in this direction as yet, but I can say
that they have come from the intuitive mystical faculty in me
which you've long derided. My experiences—both before and
after leaving the States; my reading Jung, Sartre, Old and New
Testaments, books on mysticism, Miller, Mormon literature,
book on Judaism, Biblical commentaries, William James; and*

the meeting with significant people on the road have all combined to lead me in this direction.

I am far from any clear concept of God and much that depicts God and Jesus in the Testaments displeases me and offends my sensibilities; but at this point I would say, though I may look upon it as a rash and foolish statement later, that it is very difficult for any "open" man of integrity to read the New Testament and conclude that Jesus was only a mere historical personage—no matter how poetically and lavishly described and praised. I'm not sure of your reaction to all this but somehow I can picture you thinking that old Katz has thrown in the towel, that rather than live in a painful, open universe, he has succumbed to the need for comfort and finality.

On the contrary, I perceive that this way would cause me to make a radical "about face" in my intellectual, emotional and physical approach to life—none of which I am prepared to undertake at this time. I think you were right about this trip being born of my "romantic" restlessness, but it is deepening into something far more. I think the experiences in Egypt—and especially in Israel—will be of great importance, and I look forward to the opportunity to stay put in one place where I can really do some serious thinking and reading. In a sense, I want to play Nietzsche against God, as they represent the polarities, and choose of the result of that collision as it relates to all the important life and death questions of my personal, professional and "inner" life.

On the ship from Italy to Greece I met an unpublished young (23) writer from New York, and we stayed together at the Hotel Cecil in Athens, the one Miller lauds in The Colossus, and have taken a side trip to Crete and now through Peloponnesia. He reminds me of you in many ways, and though he is very preoccupied with the problems of his life, we manage to act as sounding boards for each other. We have traveled "steerage" or deck passage everywhere, among the chickens, vats of olive oil, bags of fruit, bottles of wine and thick, gesticulating peasantry. It has been quite an experience.

Soon it will be dawn, and we will explore the temples, stadium, monuments and public buildings of Olympia as well as its famous museum. Then, after lunch, we will be off for Athens in time for my departure Wednesday for Alexandria. What awaits me there with my "mission" I do not know, but I hope my stay is brief and successful. It is almost seven months of tramping now, and I am tired and anxious to reach Israel.

If I can impose upon you once more, and if you can raise the necessary spirit, why not give Helga a ring? It's probably been a few months since you've spoken to her and a call will delight her. Best wishes to you also, you rascal, for a most creative New Year.

CHAPTER THIRTEEN

LETTER FROM SAUL GOLDMAN
December 28, 1963

I have just finished eating a huge tossed green salad with croutons and a Caesar dressing. Very satisfying. I will be writing to you at intervals in the course of the day since I will be watching the East-West game on television this afternoon.

After reading what you have to say about your mystical inclinations, I feel compelled to defend reason as man's most useful faculty. There may be very little disagreement between us, but we do not seem to communicate well with each other on this topic. One can talk about Jesus Christ as something more than a mere historical personage. Of course he is something more than that—the Christian religions have made him a symbol. And symbols have a way of getting into our nervous systems and into our dreams. I explain Jesus from a scientific (rational) point of view because I believe very strongly that that point of view best enables us to communicate effectively with each other. The fact that my point of view is scientific, however, does not mean that I am rejecting intuition—I am merely using a scientific principle to connect my intuitions and to establish a framework for acting upon them.

All of what I have just said is, of course, too general. To get anywhere at all on the topic, we would have to start off by defining "intuition" and "reason," and then we would have to discuss particular instances of the uses of the two. If you want to do this, I am willing. Tell me just what intuition is, and where it is getting you, and I'll tell you just what reason is, and

*where it's getting me. And I do feel it's getting me somewhere.
My studies in literary criticism have familiarized me with I. A.
Richards and a number of other very rational modern critics.
Reading their ideas has helped me to clarify my own position.
I am attaching a sheet which contains quotations from Rich-
ard's essay, "Science and Poetry," which expresses a world
view very similar to what I once thought yours was, but which
rejects mysticism, that is to say, the cult of one's vague feelings; the essay does not reject Feeling.*

*I ought to mention that by being abroad you missed some-
thing unlike anything members of our generation have ever before witnessed in America. I am referring to the aftermath of
the Kennedy assassination. I'm sure you were stunned by the
news too, but I wish you could have seen the effect it had on
your countrymen.*

*Helga called me on Christmas Day. We talked for about
thirty minutes. She seems to be in good mental health.*

*Scandal at Inglewood: Judy Goldstein is going around with a
Negro. I can't remember his name, but he was the tall, light-
skinned, good-looking center on the basketball team last year.*

*With high resolve to write frequently, and with eager antici-
pation of hearing your impressions of Israel, I close with my
friendliest best wishes.*

LETTER TO INGER
CAIRO, EGYPT
January 13, 1964

*I received your letter yesterday. It was very important and
sensible and not at all childish, and I will answer it seriously,
though I know you will have considerable trouble translating
my letter.*

*Unfortunately I was on a ship from Greece to Egypt during
Christmas and could not call you. I hope you will excuse me.*

You ask about the nationality of my parents. My mother was born in England and my father in Russia. Both are Jewish. If you find that confusing, you must read in an encyclopedia about the tortured wanderings of the Jews on the face of the earth, and whether being a Jew refers to one's race, religion or nationality. Few have ever agreed.

Everything you have told me about the National Council for Unmarried Mothers seems quite reasonable, and I will comply with it and go with you to the authorities when I arrive in Denmark.

You are very dear to me. I respect you greatly. You are the purest, most noble soul I know. You opened my eyes to the meaning of love by your selfless devotion to me, and I have deepest affection for you. But you must not have unrealistic expectations and hopes about me. I will love the baby, and I will always feel deeply responsible for you both—but only God knows what form our final relationship will take. What seems to be emerging from the experience of this trip is a new kind of relationship between me and the world. I started this trip because I wanted deeper, more extensive and meaningful experience; and I have found that with you and others. I can no longer consider myself an American only, but a man who has many commitments and friendships all over the world.

Concerning you: Could you be happy in a relationship with me in which we write often, I help you financially and come to see you and the baby almost every year? As I said, ours is an unusual relationship. I want to do what is right and am feeling my way. Every man hungers for the great love that will fill his inner void, and I pray that someday God will bless me with such a love. You must be prepared to face the possibility that it may happen to me tomorrow or next month or next year—either with you or someone else. On top of that, my divorce is not yet final—one must wait a year—and I suspect that Helga still loves me.

Jesus says it is a sin, an offense in the eyes of God, to put away your wife, except for the cause of adultery, and as I am

*coming closer and closer to becoming a Christian, I do not
know how ultimately I may interpret my obligations.*

*I have been changing greatly over the past few months. I
read and think constantly about God, religion and its application to my life, and so I cannot predict how the future will un-
fold for us. It was the influence of your character, your innocence, that started me thinking along these lines, and I am very
grateful to you. You must have the courage and hope to face
that open, undefined future without pressuring me or making
demands, though, of course, you have every right to! I can
promise to try to be the best man I can—but only God knows
my heart. I hope you can understand me, for there are things
that lie still deeper within me. Perhaps you can see better now
the kind of "soul mate" I need in a woman. I have not yet been
able to find her; if I have found her, I am not aware of it or of
my love for her.*

*I am pleased that you are proud your baby will have a Jew-
ish father, but what do your parents and family say about
that?*

LETTER TO HELGA
CAIRO, EGYPT
February 5, 1964 (5:00 a.m.)

*Something has been prodding me to write you, although I
keep postponing it, waiting for your letter which does not come.
Now I shall not resist the impulse any longer.*

*It is no easy matter to sever a relationship of seven years,
and I had been often occupied in the course of my trip debating the rightness of doing so. What finally decided me—that's
too strong—rather, what gave me the last assurance about the
futility of our continuing, was your recent letter. No doubt this
may perplex you a bit because in it you wrote that you were
willing to forgive me all the injuries done, forget the past, let*

*bygones be bygones, and, in general, accommodate yourself to
however changed a person you would find me.*

*It was obvious to me that such a proclamation was strictly
verbal and synthetic, because if it were real and heartfelt it
would have had to be preceded by an intense transformation of
character. I pictured you writing that statement at great cost,
through clenched teeth, as a person writes a forced confession
at gunpoint. What made it so obviously a lie was its contrast
with the balance of the letter, which was filled with same old
self-pity, resentment, sense of injury and grievance as ever.
You act and write as if I have done you some great injustice,
and now you are willing to bow in humble submission, forgive
my black deeds and receive me back. That would never work,
and it would not be long before we would be making each other
miserable again.*

*You closed your letter with the tender words "Yours for you
know what." This brought to mind recollections of our loveless,
erotic, straining wrestling matches, completely devoid of spirituality. Though I may have been a partner in that before—a
willing partner—I don't think I can do it now. Even though
you have a perfect right to be bitter about all that has taken
place, you must transcend it, or it is hopeless between us. No
amount of surface adjustment or verbal declaration will do it,
for if the resentment and bitterness lurks beneath, everything
will be poisoned. But for the change to be thoroughgoing and
real would amount to a kind of revolution of personality. If
your first thought now is "What is HE doing about HIS?" you
are just proving my point.*

*For the sake of discussion, how could this "revolution" be
achieved? (Stand back for a shock.) From my present understanding, I believe one would have to become a true believer.
Not that I have yet achieved this particular plateau of spirituality, but I do see that for you there will be no hope unless you
forgive yourself for all you've done to cause your present misery. I have absolved myself of all guilt and trust that you will*

be able to do the same through some deeper spiritual insight than you now seem to be capable of.

"Tsk . . . tsk . . . and he was such a nice Jewish boy," you say. Strangely enough, I have never been more conscious and proud of being a Jew than I am at the present moment. I see Judaism and Christianity not as opposites, but as a continuum—the latter evolving out of the former and reaching out to a deeper and loftier spiritual plain. What the full implications of this growing understanding may be for me, I do not know as yet. It means a lifetime of continual reevaluation and search, and often I am terribly perplexed, disturbed and overwhelmed and cry out for light and guidance. I am a novice at prayer, and often the words catch in my throat. I realize too, that much of what I spent my lifetime in painfully obtaining and strengthening—my pride, my intellectual arrogance, my heroic man-centered universe, my disdain for humility and meekness—will probably have to be sacrificed, and I am as yet not quite ready to do that, as you might suspect from the tone of my letter. I do not want to be a sheep like Ken Jordan, and have not yet worked out whether prostrating oneself before God means abdication of one's manhood.

I am in the process of being reborn in a tension that is at once excruciating and delightful. Wherever it leads, I have faith that it is for the better. It is too late to undo what has been done, but I will endeavor in the future to be the best man and live the most meaningful life of which I am capable. I regret what has happened to you in the process, but cannot change that now.

Perhaps you are convinced now, more than ever, that I am insane. If so, we are as far apart as ever, for I believe the root of modern man's distress and restlessness is spiritual rather than physical, although the two are intimately interrelated. Respond honestly and directly, not as you think I would like, but as you freely feel.

Yours for I don't know what.

The letter to Helga is on its way. Now I wish I had been kinder, more gentle. Can I absolve myself from guilt? There is a nagging feeling, an inner voice that points the accusing finger—at me.

CHAPTER FOURTEEN

CAIRO, EGYPT
February 24, 1964

I am writing from my small grubby room at the nearly dilap-
idated "New Hotel" in Cairo. In three days I will have been in
Egypt two months, with the prospect of remaining yet a few
more weeks before the museum's business is completed. I had
not anticipated a stay of such length, but so it goes. I expected
that my teeth would be set on edge in what I pictured to be an
extended Morocco. Instead, Cairo is quite European in its
downtown parts, and Joe, who leads the weekend Jewish services, and his circle are typically twentieth century "modern."

As a matter of fact, Egypt has little to do with my most important experience here, the considerable reading and thinking
I have done during my enforced leisure. Ordinarily, I would
have torn myself to pieces in frustration at the delays and pro-
crastinations, and jeopardized the whole mission by antagoniz-
ing an important leader of the Jewish community. Instead, I
have accepted this time as God's will, and have been reading
every book I can find—mostly on religion.

About a week after my arrival I became ill with jaundice,
and spent two weeks at the Italian Hospital—at the expense of
the Cairo Jewish Community—recovering from what was
diagnosed as hepatitis. Never have I been so near death. For
days I lay unknowing, unable to receive nourishment, my body
wracked with fever. I remember coming to my senses and
looking at my self-winding watch, only to find it had run down.
Perhaps the enforced rest was beneficial, permitting a disre-

gard for the ordinary canons of time—waking, reading or sleeping when I will, for small snatches, as the impulse takes me.

Since I was in a hospital staffed by nuns, I looked forward to a visit from the priest, in hopes of getting him to explain my New Testament and answer my innumerable questions concerning its seeming conflicts. However, he was most unresponsive when I tried to draw him into a conversation concerning the things of God, and I at last concluded he did not want to talk about the matter. Too bad, for I still have many unanswered questions. I cannot understand a Christ who would say, "Let the dead bury their dead." It seems harsh and contradictory, as do many other passages. All still remains unexplained, although I am confident that one day someone will appear with the answers that will satisfy the deeper longings of my soul.

Joe and George have been dear boys to me. Joe is highly religious, the sober, serious and responsible son who runs the shop and leads the family. His religion is more ceremonial and habitual than spiritual. He is pointed out as a "good Jew" because he knows all the services by heart. Although he is a good man, loyal and tireless in the museum's interest, he displays no sensitivity or exceptional ethical or moral feelings. On the return trip from Aswan, he instructed me not to permit anyone into our compartment when the train stopped at Luxor, although we had a few spare seats. I asked how he would like it if *we* were denied a seat, as we *had* been on the terrible journey coming south through the desert. He as much as said, "each man for himself." Later, in conversation with some of my Jewish cohorts, I raised this point and said a good Jew would make room for another, and a good Christian would give his seat to another. They thought the whole concept quite amusing.

George, the Greek, is very effusive, loud, emotional and has created a certain role for himself in the group. He is the petulant photographer, the one who must ever be beseeched, the one who bickers and argues loudly about trifles—and is loved as a kind of burly mascot. Yet in the midst of this he talks about death and is shot through with self-pity, lavishly depreciating himself. I have grown fond of both boys and am very grateful for their help.

Two months in Egypt! I have a bad cold to boot, and what feels like a dull fever, and I tossed and turned in bed this afternoon, pitying myself, picturing a serious illness coming on again, and still thousands of miles away from those who could comfort me. Reading *The Essential T. E. Lawrence* has made me somewhat ashamed of myself as I contrasted my small ills with the enormous physical adversity he had to endure. I am now thirty-five, supposedly a man, and still experiencing such pangs as I have described and lapsing into woeful melancholy about the present confusion of my life and the uncertainty of the future. It seems that by this time a man should have gained a solid footing on earth. Yet all the others I talk to and associate with are as insecure and unsure as I, although most refuse to admit it, feigning brusqueness, licentiousness, frivolity, or extreme piety.

I suppose much of what has pricked my bubble has come from the frustrations of my errand here. This morning at the Purim celebration I saw some of the Jewish leaders and spoke briefly—hurriedly in order to get my few words in—with one about the present stalemate over the shipping. I am invited to the board meeting next Wednesday when final word will be given. So I have now several days to wait again, in a kind of cancerous idleness only partially mitigated by my reading. My head is stuffed and aching, my nasal passages clogged. I feel prickly, hot and miserable and am disgusted at my physical weakness and the unreliability of my body.

To escape the confinement of my room, I am almost anxiously looking forward to the movie tonight. I suppose I'll be miserable later for having gone, but I need some distraction from my self-pity. On top of that, I must confess a touch of homesickness—a yearning for the familiar and for warmth and affection. I miss Helga tonight very much and think of her tenderly as well as of Inger and my mother. I need a woman's comfort.

February 25, 1964 (1:30 a.m.)

I've just returned from seeing *The L-Shaped Room*, which was like being hit by a blast from a double-barreled shotgun. The doctor asks "Jane" if she plans to keep the baby. If not, she will not be allowed to see it after birth for fear she will not want to give it up. I winced to see Leslie Caron kissed by another man, and breathed a sigh of relief that I was spared the torment of seeing her in greater detail in bed with him. Is it that she reminds me of some deeply imbedded prototype for which my heart aches, waits and yearns? It's as if this heart were born in me with recollections grooved into it from another experience—from a past life yet to come. There has always been in me the hungering for the piquant, oddly beautiful, soft-souled elfish quality that exudes from some women. For one such woman I know I would overturn the earth itself, and let flow the great love that has long been compacted in my heart. Will God ever bless me to find her?

Betty Friedman sees a "recurring combination and predisposition" in my involvement with women both "lonely and naive." But I think it something other than naïveté. It is to know the world and the meaning of being human and yet not to be muddied by it, nor lose the quality of spontaneity and freshness of "innocence." My perfect woman will be beyond words; my whole nature will testify to her rightness and I will be able to say for the first and last time, irrevocably, unfalteringly, "You are the one. My life, my fate, my completed self at last. Everything that I have experienced is but preparation for you. I offer myself to you, the secret most inviolable parts which I have kept locked all the years in keeping for you, only you, because what you are can understand and love me in my totality, the same totality that fits me to love you in yours."

LETTER TO INGER
CAIRO
March 1, 1964

I hope you understood my long, complicated letter and were not depressed by it. More and more I am coming to God, and with His guidance I will try to do what is right and honorable by you and the baby—but you must continue to remind yourself that this cannot include marriage.

Remember, I must be back in California by late August if I am to return to my teaching job. I realize now that I do miss my students and my work and will be happy doing God's work in the classroom. Besides, I have been without income all year, and with my obligation to you and the baby I must earn money again. I want to save enough so I can visit you and the baby every summer.

I know you must be ill in the mornings, and suffer many pains as well as doubts, uncertainties and unhappiness in general. Please forgive me for bringing all that on you. I am wiser now, but wisdom comes when it is too late.

Will it be hard for you to see me again and then go through the pain of another parting? I am not trying to back down on my promise to return to Denmark, but perhaps my coming back for a short time only would be more cruel than kind. What do you think? As long as I am able, I will not betray the promise I made you, but I wonder if you have thought all these things out.

Give my fondest regards to your family. Do any of them speak English? I am anxious to meet them.

Arthur

Another letter from Betty Friedman arrived yesterday afternoon. It was delightful—except for one ominous omission. She
wrote not a word about Helga. The silence triggered my anxiety so that I was up until 3:00 a.m. writing her and my mother.
It smells like a conspiracy of silence.

This afternoon, I contemplated spending a second year
away, in which I would have time to fathom and cultivate the
changes in me as well as to sample more fully that land which
is my original and most important destination. But my desire
for service is so strong that I cannot stay away from my teaching any longer. I will have to return in a state of incompleteness, it seems, and work out the meaning of my life day by day
in the thick of things. I now realize more clearly than ever that
every great question and vital concern is to be had and met
right where I was—the microcosm in the macrocosm—and I
do not think I will hanker again for "greener pastures."

LETTER TO BETTY
March 4, 1964

*I need not tell you that it is a different universe with God in
it. It is most deceptive: everything appears the same and yet all
is radically altered and charged with new meaning and challenge. Something larger than myself is now at the center—although it is totally indefinable. The task is still beyond my
strength and wisdom, but I am coming to find a new source of
power and light. My gifts are not my own, but fit me to take up
my "cross," not in slavish imitation of Christ, but faithfully
and honestly as He did His.*

*As you see, you were hoping for me to become a "Jew," but
I might yet "exceed" your expectation. I have had my fling at
"playing God," and what a wake of destruction, misery and
heartache I left behind me! In the extremity, I reached the bor-*

ders of my own limits, which I no longer rail against, and discovered the frontiers of a vast, illimitable land which I am beginning to explore now with tremulous, uncertain, infant's legs. My eyes seek for new signs and my ears for a whisper that comes from the deepest center, beyond the raucous clatter of the world. God has plucked me out late—slowly and gently. Were He to come in His full glory, I would roll on the floor with dazed eyes and foaming mouth, like a crazed man, ecstatic, drunk. Wisely, knowing my enthusiastic heart, He allows me yet to linger in my doubt, removing the veil ever so gradually.

This is my present human will and wisdom speaking, but if it is not God's will, I shall change my course. This problem is at the core of all my concerns, and God knows that what may be ultimately right to do is beyond the reach of my wisdom. Every prayer is filled with requests for His guidance and direction. In the months to come I will be alert for His voice. I am learning to make mine not so strident that it would drown His should it come. Besides, I have a growing feeling that one day God will invade my heart and life—totally consuming me in some capricious moment when I least suspect it.

Call me a fool, but I feel this whole experience to have been no accident and that it is not yet intended for me to know a final answer. My soul is stretched out in space (Oakland, Denmark, Paris . . .), in personal commitments (Helga, Inger, Rachel . . .), in concepts and ideals (Greek vs. Hebrew-Christian), in faith and unbelief, in moral passion and animal hunger and in many other ways. In the process of being drawn taut, I am also being made. My life was never before in so great a mess and in such a state of uncertainty as it is now. I have reached the point where I cannot say where I will be or what I will be doing next year. Almost anything is possible. Yet, I am strangely happy and confident and feel closer to the Truth than ever.

Now for the substance of your letter. You are right. Inger is hoping that when I see the child I will so love it—and her *through it—that I will be unable to leave. I have warned her not to harbor vain expectations. My heart can accommodate much, and my mind and spirit are not bound by geographical and conventional boundaries, so I am peculiarly fitted to explore and grow into this new relationship with the world. Inger, I am sure, will understand.*

I am not finished with Rachel, nor anyone, for that matter, who has meaningfully entered my heart and experience. I will never be finished with Helga—no matter what the final, legal disposition is between us. My heart remembers every joy and anguish and is often so filled with poignancy or melancholy that I scream, "Break! Break!" But I am accustomed to its weight now, and would not have it otherwise. I do not fear opening my heart to pain—I long ago resolved it is the only way. I will not take to drink or lose my sanity or any other of those dire possibilities you envision. Helga has not emasculated me, and though you and the others tremble for me, I emerge ultimately scathed, but whole and strengthened too. Keeping my word to Inger will be a terrible inconvenience, but how can I let her bear the pain of my doing alone? I intend to have a lifelong relationship with this child, and not be merely the unknown sender of periodic checks. You are right. The next parting will be painful and cruel, but she will believe my word that it is not final.

CAIRO, EGYPT
March 6, 1964

I have just returned from my 1:00 p.m. meeting, and my anger has subsided slightly. The session was stormy, full of the confusion that always abounds on Wednesday afternoon. Discussion went on in the halls and in adjoining rooms—in French, English and Arabic. The people were sitting, yelling, standing, demanding, requesting, arguing. My head is still ringing. First there was talk of a split shipment. No concurrence.

Finally it appeared that even after two months no real decision to ship had been made at all, so they must all come Sunday to the synagogue basement to see everything and decide. I am sick. I know what will happen. They will be overcome with the immensity of it. Everything is sacred to them, and they have no means of determining what I should take and what they should keep. I expect in their frustration they will give me a few minor items and leave the rest in the dusty closets to become victim of the weather or to be destroyed in the next war. God knows I have done my best to salvage these precious objects, but if His will is to be thwarted through the obstinance of man, there is nothing more I can do.

March 10, 1964

The final report. The last excruciating details. *Be patient, Katz, only one more meeting.*

By Friday evening I did not feel well and retired to the hotel rather than attend the Sabbath service with Joe as I had promised. (He thinks if I sit there something may rub off.) In a few hours, I was flushed with fever, had a terribly congested head and spent a horrible night writhing on the bed—nightmares and all. The following day I lay as dead, so weak I could not stir. I felt like all the symptoms of hepatitis had returned, and had visions of an even longer stay in the hospital this time. In my feverish musings I contemplated expiring in Israel, the promised land, so I could "enjoy" in death what had been denied me in life. Finally about 4:00 p.m. a curious servant opened my door, and I wanly beckoned him in. I must have been a sight, glistening with sweat and prostrate on a bed that looked like a battlefield. I signaled him to give me pen and paper, and I scribbled a note to the English-speaking desk clerk to call George, my Greek friend—Joe won't pick up his phone on the Sabbath—and tell him I am ill and to come over.

That night, George, Joe and the doctor arrived, and I uttered a long sigh of relief when the doctor announced I had a virus and not a recurrence of jaundice. I was to be confined to bed at least three days and to take certain drugs. But tomorrow, Sunday, was the BIG final meeting at the synagogue, and I couldn't miss that, no matter what. The doctor said, "Okay, your funeral. But hop back in bed as soon as it's over and don't tire yourself."

Sunday. The big day. I had been up since 4:00 a.m., thinking and praying. Joe called for me at the hotel, and even though I was very weak, I was able to sit quietly bundled in my coat—on a warm day—for two hours while the chief rabbi examined the old books Joe and I had pulled out of the dusty rubble of junk. Other members conferred in small groups or argued in French across the table. Joe was at my side, and I poked him in the ribs to keep me aware of all points mentioned so I could answer them when I had a chance to speak. The shipper was there, although he too was fed up with the delays, and finally after about two hours, a decision was reached. I sensed it, because the men began milling near the doors, sheepishly trying to escape as soon as the final word was given. I listened incredulously.

"You may have the books and the old torn Torah parchments and two albums of scraps."

I was aghast. "Nothing else? Nothing on the list? No documents? Manuscripts? Artifacts?"

They were firm. "NO!"

What followed I cannot report too objectively. I said many things I do not recall. It was all very heated. There was great agitation, stirring and commotion. I got into an argument with the president of the community, my chief adversary. But they were all very firm and soon dismissed, leaving me in my misery.

I reeled back to the hotel on rubbery legs, head thumping, feverish, voice gone and throat burning. I was disgusted and just didn't care any more.

March 13, 1964

I'm still in Cairo. A terrible, pounding head and earache sent me rushing to Dr. Tamecho, but no amount of pills seemed to kill the pain. By the next afternoon the pain was so acute I went with George to the doctor's office. The place was loaded with patients, but George caught the doctor on the way from one room to another, and he took a quick look at my ear. "Buy some painkiller and you'll be okay tomorrow," he said.

"You see," said George. "I told you it was nothing."

George invited me up to Denise's place—a fine, fat, lovely girl—and she made some tea for me and sent George out for some glycerin, which she later warmed in a teaspoon and poured in my ear. I had already taken four pills—six in twenty-four hours is the limit—and felt slightly pained, but cozy. The wine helped, and soon we were enjoying a good intellectual discussion over the bottle.

At 10:00 p.m. I returned to my room in hopes of a good sleep. I took my pills, read a bit and turned off the light. But sleep did not come. Instead, the pain in the ear grew worse. 1:00 a.m. 2:00 a.m. I gulped down more pills. I tried this position, that position. I got up and walked about the room. By then the pain was intense, unbearable, and sleep was out of the question. More pills. In desperation I poured nose drops in my ear in hopes of breaking up the congestion. More glycerin. Nothing helped. 4:00 a.m. 5:00 a.m. I couldn't stand it. I was going out of my skull! I dressed and rushed out into the deserted streets and found my way to Dr. Tamecho's place. All was dark. The elevator was shut down for the night. I dragged myself up four flights and pressed his buzzer.

"You must see an ear specialist," he said. "Let's see . . . the only one is at the Italian Hospital." I rested my feverish head against the cool wall, listening like a dumb animal, and then groped my way to the street and hailed a cab. Will I never leave Egypt? Now it's back to the same hospital. Oh Pharaoh, let this son of Israel go. 5:30 a.m. I had taken twelve pills and not slept in twenty-six hours—only five hours sleep in the last fifty. The doctor, a young intern, looked at my ear and told the nurse to give me a shot to calm me. I walked the corridors crying. How long this time? The pain, the pain . . . God . . . God. Images of Moses trying to fight his way out of this forsaken land flashed through my feverish mind. I decided to wait to see the ear specialist who came in at 9:00 a.m. Fifteen minutes. Half-an-hour. An hour. The pain did not cease but grew worse. The throbbing was so loud that I thought my skull would explode. By 8:00 a.m. I could not sit, but stumbled down the corridors, glancing at my watch every minute. Finally 9:00 a.m. No doctor. I wanted to scream. At 9:15 a.m. he saw me.

"Acute infection from the virus," he said. "You must have penicillin and Vitamin C shots daily, glycerin drops in the ear and hot packs continually day and night." I slumped into a chair and agreed to have myself admitted to the hospital. Almost immediately, some sister began giving me shots, tablets and a hot water bottle. Finally I fell asleep.

On the morning of the second day I felt somewhat better, though I didn't sleep too well and had stabbing pains. I asked the doctor if I could leave, and he gave permission as long as I continued the treatment.

I walked into Joe's shop at 10:30 a.m., unshaven, looking more dead than alive. He was surprised to see me and chided me for not calling. He ordered breakfast and then took my stuff back to the hotel—fifth time I've checked in. The clerk said he thought my illnesses were caused by the climate, but I told him it was the filth. I just haven't built up the immunity that comes with permanent residence in a country where people spit *everywhere*. Tomorrow, thank God, I leave for Alexandria and freedom; praying the Lord will part the seas, if necessary, to get me out of this damned place.

ALEXANDRIA, EGYPT
March 18, 1964

I arrived here yesterday with only a Torah case and a few old books in my possession. I discovered this morning I had forgotten my customs statement at the bank at Cario and spent a frantic half hour arranging to get it back tomorrow before the ship sails. I went with one of the Jewish leaders to the shipping agent who says that everything must go with me or not at all—and that it will take fifty pounds to grease his palm. I was also advised not to go to Cyprus, nor to risk taking the items with me, as I was probably on the blacklist due to the length of my stay and my activities. They are waiting only for an opportunity to create an incident and will be watching to see what I attempt to take with me when I leave the country. So, I am trapped either way. The sea before me, and the Egyptians behind me. I shall continue my plans forward, feeling that nothing could be worse than my experiences of bondage in Egypt. I shall trust God to deliver me from whatever wrath there may be to come.

CHAPTER FIFTEEN

JERUSALEM
March 29, 1964
LETTER TO SAUL GOLDMAN

Please forgive this long delay. I arrived in Israel a few days ago and was met with the accumulated mail of months, not the least of which was Helga's divorce papers.

Jerusalem seemed to be the appropriate place to be for Pass-over—Easter, too, really—so I hurried over here from Tel Aviv in time to arrange to attend a Seder at Kibbutz Ramal Rachel on the Israeli-Jordan frontier, the kibbutz famous for its heroic role in the defense of Jerusalem in '48. It was a most impressive evening, and I was touched by the communal singing inter-spersed throughout the ceremony, which made me strangely aware and proud of my Jewishness.

Nothing could have been more inauspicious than my first day in Israel. I had to redeem two small suitcases which had been stored at the Haifa customs for eight months, and was led on a nightmarish, bureaucratic chase for seven exhausting hours as if I had been following a demonic script collaborated on by Kafka, Huxley and Durrell. When done, I had a sheaf of papers—fifteen in all—stamped, signed and countersigned by more officials and clerks than it took to process me into the army for two years. I stayed the night in Tel Aviv and left the following morning for Jerusalem. En route we passed over one stretch of winding road where burned-out armored cars and half-tracks have been left alongside as reminders of the price paid for nationhood.

Jerusalem itself is lovely, the old and the new coexisting harmoniously because almost all the buildings are constructed of the same local, reddish stone. I love most the area about Mt. Zion and its view of the Old City where I really felt myself to be on holy ground. My health is still not quite right, and I was lucky to find a room for one dollar a night. My food runs about two dollars a day, so I will linger here for a week or so to rest up before I start tramping about the country.

Odd, but I must confess that the sight of the divorce papers gave me a bit of a jolt. In the light of the spiritual changes in me, I had almost contemplated giving it another go, but my selfish desire for freedom won out, so I signed and notarized the pages and sent them off. No sooner had I done so than I received a cablegram from Helga urging me not to delay, so I am relieved that she wills it also. I suppose it is coming none too soon as I am about to be a father in June by a girl in Denmark, and if Helga ever found out about that it would probably kill her. I am trusting you to tell no one, for I have confidence only in you and Betty. Miracles aside, there is no possibility of my marrying this girl. She is as true a heart and simple a soul as can grace this earth, but an unlettered small-town girl. Her English is abominable and she labors days to read my most simple letters. However, she loves me as nobly and unselfishly as ever I've been loved. Our coming together was pure innocence. I slept with her once and bang! After seven childless years with Helga I have helped create a new life. This strange, intense, loving girl, who would follow me anywhere, will not have me if I do not love her and does not even want to encumber me financially. She asks only that I be with her when the baby is born, which of course, I have promised and will do. She floods me with letters and packages, and the five letters awaiting me here told of her growing pains, of life stirring, of fears of death and ostracism, of the uncertain future—all of which tear at my heart and make the pathos of this reality more and more apparent and immediate. How it will be resolved I do not know.

I cannot marry her—it would be a cruel absurdity. Yet is it enough to be a father by correspondence? This is but one of the many tensions stretching me taut, out of which only God can fathom what will come.

Strangely, I am not depressed but acutely hopeful—a state which can be explained only in relation to the profound interior changes in me. Of this I had hoped to write you at length in response to your remarks about "human reason," but look how much space I've taken merely bringing you up to date with the most superficial account of recent events.

Actually, it is something that does not lend itself to systematic exposition, least of all in my present foggy condition, and especially to one as cynical, analytical and critical as yourself. There is, it seems to me, a far deeper order of truth that is accessible only by an affirmative act of faith which requires a belief in the intangible—an act which one's reason will not allow him to enter into without a willingness to risk a kind of self-annihilation. There is a hierarchy in which reason, aesthetics and ethics have their irreplaceable spheres but there is a crowning light above them all giving them an utterly profound, eternal meaning, and this is the spiritual. Without this, any or all of the three can become another form of escape from the deepest commitment to life as we see it, for example, in the academic life.

Lest you think that poor Katz, browbeaten by life, is going soft, I assure you that all this, far from being a source of benign comfort, creates, instead, perpetual existential tensions in which faith is ever at war with doubt, and the implications of that faith at war with one's vanity, self-seeking and desires. Kierkegaard calls faith "a paradoxical relationship to the paradoxical." I see now that this leap over the confines of what we know is the ultimate act of transcendence that at once liberates, transforms and vitalizes the individual. Without it, our reservoir of spirituality becomes a weighty load and irritation. Neglected long enough, it is often deceptively perverted into other forms, which, no matter how we try, cannot be requited or satisfied. Anyway, this is the direction in which my search for the authentic self is taking me. You will probably consider this an evasion, a flight from the bitter, uncompromising truths revealed by reason, and the last refuge of a man who cannot accept reality for what it is. But tell me, Saul, who do you know who was better equipped than I to live in and accept that reality manfully? My life is nothing if not a series of affirmative leaps, of the courage to risk, of the seeking for the core, no matter how hard its meaning. Who was better made to live in a world without meaning, and to create it, and supply it if possible? I say all this without vanity, and I believe God has sought me out, or made it possible for me to find Him because of these qualities rather than for the lack of them.

The great need in the world is for the spirit of healing and reconciliation which no institutional arrangements can provide. It must come from the hearts of men who have shifted the center of their lives outside themselves, and who are not as tempted to grasp when they accept this life in the context of eternity.

Your insurance business sounds like a good deal. I have always suspected you to be a frustrated money-maker, and have no doubts about your success. I'm going to try to talk you into teaching again, where you belong, which may work better now if you've got this extra on the side that requires perhaps only part-time maintenance.

Sorry for this sketchy, rambling letter. Don't worry, there's still too much of the old Katz to become the kind of Christian fanatic that Ken Jordan is.

Your buddy,
Art

JERUSALEM
April 3, 1964

What can I say of it? I have been exposed to dialogues, monologues and polemics with the ultra-orthodox of the Mea

Shearim, the orthodox section of Jerusalem, an orthodox professor of the Jewish law, Dr. Kohn, and a saintly young Jew who was turned to his own faith from a secular career by the attraction of Christianity. I have been called evil and dangerous, foolish and unreasonable and admonished to spend all my time studying the Talmud or turning to the "sources."

I had been here just a few days when I met Ben Shaw again. We sailed from New York together nine months ago, and since coming to Jerusalem, he has become an orthodox Jew. He wore a yarmulke when I saw him on the streets, and we threw our arms about each other. He shared what had happened to him spiritually, and I told him something of my search, and the inner revelations I have been receiving, triggered by the pressure of outer circumstances. I told him I felt I was literally being pursued by this Jesus of the New Testament. He was shocked, but considered me a challenge, and put me up in his dormitory at the Hebrew University, where I have remained for several days now.

What time I have not been talking and arguing with the students and professors at the University I have been reading books on Christianity, books on Mormonism—despite my pugnacious feelings towards Britt's religion. I am still so intrigued by her that I am willing to exhaust every source to learn more of what she believes. And I have been reading books by Jewish writers (Kaufmann and Buber) shoved at me by Ben who's deliberately and desperately trying to persuade me away from the road to Christianity. Through it all, however, I continue to see the beauty and depth of the New Testament, which, in my opinion now, is the greatest of all books.

"Arthur, did you think for a moment you could fool me? You're a sophomore now and you ought to have enough sense to realize I can recognize a plagiarized piece of writing when I see one. You get an F on this report, and if you do it again you flunk the course."

I was stunned! This presuming high school teacher had assigned us book reviews, and now accuses me of copying the one I had written. She thinks I can't do quality work because I cut up in class. She doesn't know I've been reading stuff on my way to school on the subway—stuff she can't even understand: Nietzsche, Schopenhauer, Wolfe.

So, I pick up my things and leave high school. Let the other kids scratch their heads over final exams. I'm going to read. I'm like a great pore, sweating, exuding, pulsating with the concepts that come from the pages of the books, transforming them into experiences of my own.

I'm like Thomas Wolfe, who loved books yet was intimidated by them. I walk into a library and am mesmerized by the tens of thousands of volumes, each crammed with knowledge, waiting to be absorbed. Books hold the key to learning, learning the key to knowledge and truth, and knowledge and truth the key to life. I shall search until I know the truth and the truth shall set me free.

One of the most enlightening sessions I have spent in Jerusalem was in the presence of Dr. Kohn, famed and honored professor of the Jewish law and an authority on the Talmud. It was highly illuminating, and helped me discern some of the differences between Judaism and Christianity. Ben had arranged for Dr. and Mrs. Kohn to invite me to dinner, and the evening was as fine an expression of Judaic life as is possible among the Israeli today. Theirs was a home of tranquility, peace, genuineness and love.

Kaufmann says that ritual provides occasions when one can regularly listen for the Voice that one is otherwise prone to forget. This was brought vividly to my mind when, during the long prayer of thanks at the conclusion of the Sabbath meal, I found I "had time" to make my own prayerful thanks which otherwise would never have occurred to me. The fact that I did not listen to the intonations of the professor, but rather constructed my own prayer of thanksgiving and praise did not seem particularly significant at that time, but now symbolizes something deeper than I imagined.

At one point during the long meal, Mrs. Kohn, a very charming and gracious woman, described a situation in which she and Dr. Kohn could not eat the meal especially prepared for them even though it was kosher because it *wasn't kosher enough!!* To cushion my shock that Jews can be divided even among themselves because of uncompromising observances, Dr. Kohn said it is necessary to preserve the identity of the Jewish people. I replied, "I hope I am not blaspheming, but there are some things more important than the preservation of the Jewish people as Jews in name." This question of form versus essence was the core of all the conversation that evening.

Ben says that the adherence to ritual observance is necessary in order to plant the seed of piety, even though at first the forms are senseless. He also says that the forms must be absolute (e.g., Sabbath observances) or they will in time be whittled down to where they become nonexistent. I argued that by nature, experience and temperament I prefer the life that is open-ended, lived in a state of prayerful tension, rather than in constant subservience to a body of laws.

In all these talks I've been reminded again of the eminent practicality and this-worldliness of conventional Judaism, as opposed to the antimaterialism of Christianity. I'm beginning to see that the ultimately important things of this world cannot be achieved except by men who renounce this world. I am at the point where I would like to consider both faiths true and valid. Buber, in *The Way of Man,* suggests that any man can approach God as long as his approach is sincere. Despite my desire to accept this, I hear the Jesus of the New Testament saying, "I am the way, the truth and the life. No man cometh to the father but by me." Is Jesus right or is Buber? Dr. Kohn unhesitatingly says Buber.

At the dinner table I used the analogy of a relay race in which each member of the team is peculiarly equipped for the part he plays in passing the baton to the other until the finish line is reached. I suggested that Judaism was the first runner and Christianity the anchor man—but was met by a barrage of objections. I tried also to describe the dimension of faith in which reason must be transcended to appropriate the "absurd," but Kohn scoffed at this, praising Judaism as "rational."

·A tense moment occurred during our dinner conversation when Dr. Kohn asked me about my plans. I said, "Well, I'm going from here to Denmark." He asked me why, and I answered frankly, "I made a girl pregnant there, and I promised to be with her at the time of the child's birth."

All conversation ceased as if I had pulled a switch! I looked around the table, and everyone was busy cutting chicken or shoveling food into his mouth, wiping his lips with a napkin or reaching for his wineglass. Where moments before I had been the center of the conversation, now I suddenly didn't exist. The confrontation of this "sinful" reality of life was so painful that the entire group simply refused to face it. Even Dr. Kohn looked shocked and horrified, and suddenly shifting mental gears and clearing his throat, asked Ben some question in an entirely different vein.

I was shocked also. Here is a deep dilemma in my life. It is a moral situation that is literally choking me to death. I did not intend to reveal it, but now that it is out I had hoped that this great master of the law of God could give me some insight. Here was an authority on the Torah—a representative of the best scholarship available in Judaism, and I wanted to learn his opinion, based on God's law. What is the wisdom of Judaism as applied to this situation? But he didn't say a word, simply changed the subject, and the meal continued on as if I had not been there. I learned a great deal from the silence around me!

On the way home, Ben admonished me for being crude, with no regard for the sensibilities of my hostess. Again I felt the deception of this world in shielding ourselves from the ugly, the distasteful. A quiet fury boiled within me as I saw we were playing with shadows rather than substances. What we ought to do, I told Ben, is use the materials of our lives and not fear standing naked before each other. He thought these matters personal and private. He even went so far as to say that *anyone* of cultural taste, even a Christian, would have been shocked by my brashness. I shrugged him off, classifying his definition of cultural as synonymous with "cowardly."

I have learned something of the inadequacy of the law, the inadequacy of being an expert, of having a well-ordered life within and still not coming to grips with the root issues. Professor Kohn was completely unequipped to offer advice in my situation with Inger, or to offer commiseration—the milk of human kindness. All I received—even though it was dished out with dignity and restraint—was moral indifference, and in his silence, I sensed the inadequacy of such a stance in regards to my situation. And my situation, although unique to me, is in its essence, classic and universal to all men. I wonder how today's classic Christian would have acted in response to my need. How would Christ have reacted?

Last night's orthodox service to which Ben took me was most impressive, yet in all these confrontations I have come away feeling that in the message of the New Testament I see more of the reconciling and healing spirit that the world needs. There is a tendency for the law to become an end in itself, and for men to be occupied with its letter rather than its spirit; and that it is only through the loving heart that good can flow. Further, that ritual and legal observances on the part of the Jew are divisive and tend to alienate those whom we are supposed to bring to God by our example, i.e., Mrs. Kohn's reference to the meal not kosher enough for them to eat.

April 4, 1964

I've just finished reading Kaufmann's *The Faith of a Heretic*. I'm impressed that Judaism accepts a man's nature as it is, while Christianity attempts to transform it.

Ben said, "Art, why disavow your own faith? It's wonderful that you are sensing the presence of God and coming out of your atheism, but why embrace something that is alien?" I had no answer, and he countered with, "How much of your religion do you really know?" I had to admit I didn't know much. Like most Jewish boys I had been only superficially indoctrinated for the purposes of the Bar Mitzvah, and had later rejected the entire scope of Judaism as irrelevant.

I wanted to write my own speech for the Bar Mitzvah, but the rabbi objected. I was disgusted with the artificiality of it all, even as I sang my portion of the Haftorah—"Blessed be He who has relieved me from the responsibility of this child's doing."

It was a regular Sabbath service, which lasted almost three hours. I stood straight, erect, feigning joy with mock smiles. Inside I wanted to cry—or giggle. But out there was the beaming face of my mother, for whom I was willing to go through the religious motions as an accommodation—willing to play the little game in order to be free.

After it was all over, we went home to a table spread with food and wine. There was a big joke about the fountain pens. I had received several as gifts. I left the old synagogue chanting not, "Today I am a man," but, "Today I am a fountain pen."

Last night I called Martin Buber on the phone. He has retired from the University, but still holds preeminence as the greatest of all Hebrew theologians. Having read his book on Judaism and Christianity and feeling the seeming conflict between the two ways in my own life, I hoped he could help me.

His voice was weak, but he granted me a few minutes, telling me the old tale about Rabbi Izik's dream of the treasure buried by the bridge at Prague. "There is something that can be found only in one place. It is a great treasure, which may be called the fulfillment of existence. The place where this treasure can be found is the place on which one stands."

I was impressed and grateful for this insight, and lay for an hour or so after the conversation trying to fathom the depth of what this great sage had said in those few words.

I sense here in Jerusalem a unique kinship with the city. I know little about its past or the Old Testament heroes. I am a seeker rather than a Jew or Christian. What connection do I have with this land of nomads where my people were shepherds, with this arid, dry wasteland, I who grew up in the midst of steel and brick? But here is something strangely familiar, as though I have been here before, as though this is actually my homeland, and for the first time in my life I am "returning." I sense it in the topography of the land, in the people themselves. Perhaps it is the indigenous golden rock, the bare hills, the sun glinting off the shimmering pinkish houses and roofs of mosques and churches. For reasons beyond my comprehension Jerusalem is indeed the city of gold.

CHAPTER SIXTEEN

HADASSAH HOSPITAL
JERUSALEM
April 7, 1964

Sitting here waiting to be called for a checkup on my ear, I watch the women sitting opposite me and notice that I am no longer offended by spindly legs and misshapen bodies. My "Greek" love of beauty had made me contemptuous of the unaesthetic in the past, but I must have moved to Buber's view that there is purpose and sanctity in God's diversity. Having spindly legs is part of the actuality to be accepted and worked through in a person's route to God. It offers, as does beauty, a set of factors to be thrown into the dialectical hopper.

Today I read from the prophet Micah: "Do justice, love mercy, walk humbly with thy God." How lauded this and other moral prescriptions such as the "golden rule" are. I'm reminded of Sartre's statement that no religion or moral code can answer the deepest, most perplexing, human problems. For example, what is "justice," "mercy"?

For four years I've poured myself out without reserve as a classroom teacher. I take it seriously, Saul says too seriously. My classroom is a miniature universe. Every great force, every passion that moves the world is alive in this room. But I am in a constant state of consternation in giving grades. I marvel at my colleagues who seem to do it effortlessly. But I know that to give a student who expects an A, a B, could imperil his chances for a scholarship, even affect his career. A failure can mean that a student, instead of spending the summer working to earn money for college, will be in school taking history over again. I find myself in the position of God, able to determine the destiny of my pupils by the stroke of a pen. I tremble at this kind of power—when I am unable to distinguish justice from mercy.

How do Micah's statement and the golden rule answer the question of the morality of premarital sex? Is violence classified as self-defense or self-interest, e.g., the militant state of Israel? The inadequacy of absolutes is revealed in "Thou shalt not murder," for example, "except or if—" "Thou shalt not lie— except for necessary 'white lies'." Even more difficult is the command "not covet," as if one can rule out envy or desire from the human heart by simply willing it. Perhaps the most satisfying answer is the New Testament fulfillment of love AS law—which assumes that no evil can flow from the truly loving heart. "Therefore if thine enemy hunger, feed him; if he thirst, give him drink . . . be not overcome of evil, but overcome evil with good." The evil that flows from excess of "mother love," for example, is not really love for the child at all, but self-love parading as concern for the other. For moral decisions to be forged in the crucible of the loving heart is excruciating, painful, requiring overwhelming responsibility in each situation if we are mindful of our fallibilities. The necessary humility and strength can be drawn only from faith in God. We are helped also if our understanding of the world is essentially tragic, so that we do not expect every solution to be "happy."

Since Jesus was the only "perfect" man, and therefore the only one able to keep the golden rule or ten commandments, then only HE could live up to these precepts. The rest of us are doomed to a life of striving for perfection, yet never reaching it—doomed to the frustration of the impossible goal. It seems that the only way possible for mortals to achieve a command of self, to be able to conquer desire and move on to the deeper things of God would be for Jesus Himself to actually come and abide in each of us. That still seems to me impossible.

LETTER TO INGER
JERUSALEM
April 9, 1964

I received your very nice letter a few days ago, but have been too busy to write you until now. I stayed ten days in Jerusalem, which is a very beautiful city, and will leave from this kibbutz tomorrow to visit another part of this wonderful country. Do you know what a kibbutz is? It is a farming community where everyone works together without receiving any wages. Everyone shares alike, eats the same food, wears the same clothing and has the same homes. It is a kind of communism but very democratic and idealistic. The children in some kibbutzim do not sleep with their parents, but have their own place with nurses and teachers, joyfully seeing their parents a few hours in the evening and on the Sabbath.

These people have taken a wasteland and created a miracle in it by their sweat and devotion. They are strong, proud and resourceful. It reminds me that I am born a Jew, and perhaps have a greater responsibility to help create this Jewish homeland than to return to the United States for my service. Still, I will return to California for at least one year, and then decide what to do about the future. Again I ask you, "Do your parents know that I am Jewish?" What do they say about that? Have you told them the truth, that they cannot hope for me to marry you, and that it is not as you said to them, that you refuse to go to California? I tell you that unless you tell them the full truth, I will not come in June. I do not want any misunderstanding and false hopes.

You are torturing yourself foolishly to dream of marriage, Inger. If it comes, it will be God's miracle, but you must not desire it or think of it or expect it. My every prayer is filled with

*requests for His guidance and will in this matter, and I have
put myself in His hands. Our whole story has been unusual,
and perhaps some unusual relationship, which neither one of
us can picture or understand now, is to come of it. I am very
pleased that you are taking English lessons, as nothing would
be possible if we could not at least communicate with each
other.*

*Our differences have to do with education, background, ex-
periences and tastes that for the most part cannot be taught or
made up, and the failure of my marriage has taught me clearly
how important it is that a couple have these in common. No
matter how much you may desire it otherwise, life has formed
us differently. There is no reason we cannot be friends, but it
would be suicidal to consider anything more.*

*I am writing you simply now, and look how you must strug-
gle and labor to understand me. What if I were to write you my
deepest thoughts and concerns? Even most of my American
friends and colleagues cannot understand me, though we have
had comparable educational backgrounds. I am a very complex
person, and though you love me, you barely know me at all,
and perhaps never can. I lived with my wife for seven years,
and cannot think of another person who knows me less. Somewhere in the world is a woman who can understand me and un-
lock my soul and give me peace. I must wait for her—no matter
how long—and perhaps it is that God does not intend for me to
be so blessed, but to be His servant only. Then you must be to
me one who loves me but cannot have me, content to share me
with God. I will not run from my responsibility, but that does
not mean that I feel my responsibility is to marry you. I am
very sorry, but you must not expect that. I will not make a second big mistake in my life.*

*I tell you all this now so that you may prepare yourself for
the fact that I must leave Denmark in July. I am depending on
you to be brave and composed, or else I will regret having come
back. By now, you know that my promises are good, and that I*

*honor my word—so you can take comfort when I say you will
see me again, as often as I can possibly make it. But for God's
sake, do not dream of "miracles." Be practical and sensible: expect nothing, except what I have promised you, and you will
not be disappointed. If this coming visit of mine is pleasant and
not hysterical, I will look forward to returning to you and the
baby again and again. Do not spoil it by foolish expectations or
overemotional partings.*

KIBBUTZ YOD MORDECHAI
April 10, 1964

First impressions: A working utopia! Swimming pool, recre-
ation room and theatre with removable roof. Every imaginable
accommodation—fine housing, clothing, food. Everyone gets
three dollars a month regardless of his job, and the most ex-
alted have to take their turn once a month waiting on tables in
the mess hall. Children have their own quarters, and see their
parents for a few hours in the evening, and, as Yitzcoch said:
"They love them for themselves and not for what they can give
them. Since the parents provide nothing, there is no envy or
competition, and the kids don't have the 'gimmes.'" They
work from one to three hours a day, from the ages of fourteen
up, and all the kids have their own small farm, and even sell
chickens and geese for money that goes to a special fund.
From what I have seen, the kids are completely unselfcon-
scious and drape themselves about anyone. This is a new breed
being born here—resourceful, tough, capable, but perhaps
lacking in the sensitivity and acute self-consciousness and in-
trospection that marked the Jew of old.

What a diversity of faces and types! Some more typically
American than a native Iowan! What seems to be lacking is
joy. Is it that this new type is quieter, less exuberant than the
old Jew? It seems to the casual observer that the kibbutz is for

them a place where they live, eat, sleep and work privately in a socialist setup. There is no outward ethos, and people drift in and out of the dining hall for meals—a place where they come only to be fed. There is nothing spiritual, intellectual, ritual or ceremonial in evidence, and it seems that something of this kind is necessary to provide the dynamic qualitative elements to transform a mechanically successful social scheme into the life deeply lived.

As impressive, utterly democratic, etc., as it all is—and very successful financially, too—for me, it is not "real" life, but a kind of make-believe, far removed from the vital conflicts of this world. Yet, it is an experiment that ultimately may provide the model and inspiration to resolve human conflict—the social variety, at least.

The kibbutz is not only community, farm and factory, but a fortress as well. In the tradition of the "minute men," each man is trained and has his position should war come. Atop the hill a beautiful memorial mound is laid out for those heroes who died in the defense of the kibbutz in 1948 when everything was completely destroyed. It is amazing what has been built up since, and except for the destroyed water tower left as a monument, there is nothing suggestive of anything but tranquility. Flowers, trees and greenery are everywhere, and it is hard to believe that less than twenty years ago there was nothing but sand dunes—a real testimonial to human ingenuity and sweat. Everything is extremely modern and up-to-date, both in the homes and fields. Cows are milked electrically, chickens hatched artificially and scientific techniques prevail everywhere. One sees few if any "fat-bottoms," and often you see the rugged, hard-nosed types who occasionally sport the abbreviated handlebar mustache so popular with young Israelis. During the Martyr's Day Ceremony yesterday I could not take my eyes off the people, especially the kids, who remained patient through the long, tedious speeches.

April 11, 1964

Still at Kibbutz Yod Mordechai. Yitzcoch, a Jewish cowboy, took me this morning to see the cattle turned out to graze. It was an inspiring sight to see this boy in the saddle, assured and commanding. We had a long chat afterwards, in which I was able to get a real sense of what an Israeli youth is and what this country means to him. His devotion to the kibbutz and to Israel are the primary unqualified loyalties of his life. However satisfying his work is, he knows that he cannot be happy short of "being a full man" and, as he put it, he is more than a farmer and wants to learn about the world. When I suggested that the people here lacked joy and were not close to one another, cooperating merely for material need, he walked over to a cactus and spoke of the sabra, prickly outside and sweet inside, and indicated that the Israeli is a new type in the world. Unlike the traditional notion of the effusive and emotional man, this is a man of outward reserve, but filled with commitment to all his comrades.

Students call teachers by their first names, and soldiers are punished by two hours hard labor for calling an officer by his rank. I asked why a student should be concerned with subjects that don't relate to his work and was told of an old Israeli saying that "man does not live by bread alone." More and more I realize that no amount of reading could have really shown me what this country means. One must walk its fields, see the transformed wastelands, marvel at the accomplishments and gauge its spirit through men like Yitzcoch.

Religion, in the common sense, touches these people not at all. Yitzcoch tried to explain that his very life is in helping create and reinforce a Jewish state. For Jews throughout history, dispersed in other lands, religion was the mode through which their identity as Jews was maintained. Now to devote one's life to the Jewish state is the daily observance—a kind of secular religiosity. He observes Pesach (Passover), Suc-

coth (Tabernacles), and other religious holidays as a seasona
festival, just as his forefathers did in this land thousands o
years ago, believing that Israel is literally the "kingdom o
God" here on earth.

I asked him about God. "Man is his own god," he said. He
feels that every person born into this world represents some
thing new, something that never existed before, something
original and unique. It is the duty of every person in Israel to
know and consider that he is new and unique in the world and
that there has never been anyone like him. He agrees with
Buber that, if there is a world to come, he will not be asked
"Why were you not like Moses?" but rather, "Why were you
not Zuaya (yourself)?"

BEERSHEBA
April 15, 1964

Tomorrow is the big day, the sixteenth anniversary of Is
rael's independence, and already the crowds are so thick in the
streets that auto traffic is almost impossible. The hotel is full to
overflowing, so it seems a miserable, chilly night ahead for me
"sleeping" on the grass. One cannot help but be attracted by
the many beautiful people around. There's hardly a dull face
in the crowd, and the number of startling physiques—male
and female—is amazing. These people are strong and vigorous
Conspicuous often by contrast is the American Jewish tourist
with misshapen body and varicose-veined legs.

And what beauty in the countryside! I had never before
seen anything quite like it. From Beersheba to the Dead Sea I
rode for an hour or so through flat, pleasant, shrubby desert
and then, quite suddenly, the bus descended sharply over a
winding road which opened up a panoramic vista that made
me catch my breath at its stark power. Against a pale blue sky
stretched a treeless, salmon-tinted mountain range, forming
the backdrop for the Dead Sea—itself a quilt of shimmering

blues and greens set off by a yellow ochre, then sandy-colored expanse of beach. What an exquisite and subtle palette! It made designations like "blue" and "green" and "yellow" seem crass and vulgar. My eye absorbs, but my hand rebels at writing the description so indescribable was it. In a few minutes the bus was at the lowest point on earth. Skirting the sea in the foreground were low, pock-marked hills, surely scraped out by the fingers of God in a paroxysm of judgment as if He had said, "There! Let's see if anyone dare grow anything here now!"

In this waste from the raw, long dead ashes of fire and brimstone, great chemical plants pierced the skyline. The vegetation was nothing but a few pitiful shrubs.

As the bus continued through the salt hills, on the skyline a pale green tint appeared and then suddenly, lush verdure, thick crops, and we were at Engedi.

Leaving the bus for an overland tour on foot, I separated myself from the group, and finding a path partially cut out of rock, I climbed upward into the very heart of this fiercely beautiful country. In a short while I came to the source of a small stream—a gush of pure water dropping straight out of the face of the rock cliff forty feet above. Following the winding stream down, I came across a succession of pools, ideal for trout, and selected one hidden enough to permit me a brief swim in the skin. It was the closest I had ever been to Eden, gliding about for that short while in the purest water while the fountain from above gushed into the natural stone basin. I came out just in time to miss the caravan of American tourists, their bodies unaccustomed to the strain, puffing and stumbling awkwardly in fashionable shoes unfit for the outing. Fortunately I'd had my moment when standing in the sun drying. Completely naked to the warm air and light, pleased with the firmness of my body, I felt at one with nature and myself. It was a quiet moment of joy that continues, hours afterwards, to uplift me.

KIBBUTZ LAVI
April 18, 1964

It will be difficult to summarize my two days of discussion with Danny Canfield, Harvard law-school graduate and American expatriot who turned to orthodoxy and came to Israel to live in a kibbutz. Every aspect of community life is rigidly based upon the exacting requirements of the law, which prescribes not only the type of crops to be grown, but the system of tithing in practice at the time of the Temple. For these people, the law is no "yoke," but a holy commandment to be followed to the letter, irrespective of the inconveniences or even seeming purposelessness. I had no idea how fantastically detailed and elaborate it is—let alone the vast literature that surrounds it. In his view, the Jew is involved in a great cosmic drama, mostly beyond his limited comprehension, and his single, unswerving duty is to fulfill the law through study and daily observance.

He tried to explain his views more fully to me. "If orthodox practices make for divisiveness in the family of men—so be it. If they violate one's sense of justice or compassion, that too must be subjugated to the law. All of that reflects man's puny standard and not God's—whose will is explicit both in the written and oral law. Devotion to God is not necessarily served by service to men."

All he said seemed to me the antithesis of Jesus' injunction, "Inasmuch as ye have done it unto the least of these my brethren, ye have done it unto me."

I quoted Amos's prophetic cry: "I hate, I despise your feast days . . . though you offer me burnt offerings and your meat offerings I will not accept them . . . but let judgment run down as waters, and righteousness as a mighty stream." Danny interprets that to mean that ritual is not necessarily offensive in itself, but only when separated from man's daily righteousness. As to the Christian allegation of the root sin of pride inherent in one's observance of the law, he said, "Yes, if one looks down and sees how far he's come; but a Jew is always admonished to look up to see how far he has yet to go, and is reminded in his daily prayers of his vain efforts and of the human limitations of even the most holy Jewish heroes. Nothing but all-out effort will do, and, like Abraham, we must give up everything and wander in the desert if it is so commanded us." Yet I sense all this is done in man's effort, and I am overwhelmed at the way Danny looks upon God as the One who set the wheels in motion centuries ago and who has now divorced himself from the human race, leaving it up to mankind, Jewry, to either get the task done by obedience to the minute details of the Law or to accept the responsibility for failure.

That night, as I lay unsleeping on my hard cot, my mind kept trying to force me to take personal inventory. Am I being judgmental? Am I accusing Danny, Professor Kohn—all Jews for that matter—of compartmentalizing the law, separating righteousness and justice from their own personal lives, while I am living the biggest lie of all, haunted by thoughts of Helga and Inger and my responsibilities in these matters? The thought remains like a pebble in my shoe, irritating every step.

How does life here differ from what I observed at Yod Mordechai? First a closer kinship is more evident among all the families here and on the Sabbath everyone eats at the same time and follows the meal with prayers and singing. Danny, Johnny and his wife, Essie, all assured me of the fine quality of these people and their warm enduring relationships.

Abraham Joshua Heschel, in *God in Search of Man*, says:

"It is one thing to be for a cause and another thing to be in a cause. Asserting 'I believe in . . .' will not make a person a Jew, just as asserting 'I believe in . . . the United States of America' will not make a person an American. A citizen is he who accepts obligations. Thus our relationship to God cannot be expressed in belief but rather in the accepting of an order that determines all of life."

It was interesting in this particular orthodox kibbutz how the older kids took an amazing and fond interest in the younger. I asked Moshe, my young host, if his time would not be more profitably spent in the study of literature than in certain remote portions of the Talmud. He replied, "Perhaps, but how can one compare the works of man with that which is Divine and Eternal?"

How indeed? My question is: Is the whole body of the law divine, or is some of it the expression of that peculiar Jewish genius for splitting hairs which accounts for the voluminous works of the rabbis and sages throughout the generations? Is that God's word too?

The crux of the matter and my conclusions are:

(1) I cannot conceive of a God who would stoop to lay out every detail, every ten handsbreadth, of the law. (Danny: "It is not for you to conceive the God that would suit YOUR fancy.")

(2) What is one's duty to God? To serve one's fellowman or the Law? (Danny: "It is not for YOU to define what YOU think your duty is, but to follow what HE has said your duty is —which is obeying the letter of the law, both written and oral.")

(3) If history is the playing out of God's plan, how is man free to will in his life?

(4) Love cannot be commanded but must be elicited freely and spontaneously. (Danny: "Love, like all other emotions, must be summoned up by an act of the will.")

(5) I distinguish between the act of evil and the evildoer. Danny, in an emotional burst shouted, "Evil should be stamped out, killed!" He cited Hitler to try to win my obvious assent. I continued, "No man is so evil he should be crushed— not even Hitler—but all men should be treated as creatures of God and, if necessary, confined, but not stamped out along with their evil. It's one thing to hate sin—quite another thing to hate the sinner. In New Testament teaching one is asked to

embrace the sinner, and Jesus said he had not come to minister to the healthy, but the sick; whereas in your Judaism, at best, the sinner is spurned." Danny disagreed violently, gingerly fingering his carbine at the same time, as though he were anxious to "do battle for God."

CHAPTER SEVENTEEN

I picked up your letter last Friday on my way through Tel Aviv, after completing a brief swing through the south end of the nation with short stays at Beersheba, Eilat, the Dead Sea and a miraculous gushing oasis in that barren waste called En-gedi. Since then I've stayed two days at an Orthodox kibbutz and the balance of the time at a couple of youth hostels near Tiberias on the Sea of Galilee. Tomorrow I leave for Safad, an ancient town of mystical sects and now an artists' colony, and thereafter will continue my journey northward. For the last two days I have traveled with two Swiss boys training for the priesthood, both of whom are good company.

I must say I loved your chatty letter—even the bit about the danger of becoming a religious charlatan. After being occasionally immersed in a bit of dung, which is unavoidably a partial product of the spiritual quest, your not-taking-life-so-seriously tone was just the corrective I needed.

Despite my nightmarish first day in Israel, I have grown very fond of this country. Physically, it offers a kind of subtle beauty that seeps into one's soul. I have always thought myself a man of mountains, trees and lush greenery—quite hostile to deserts. Yet, I found the trip through the Negev impressive, and the Dead Sea area powerfully stirring. It seems as if God had gone berserk there, toppling boulders and gouging out canyons in white-lipped fury. As for the human landscape, it is more

*impressive still: a new, rugged, resourceful, unsentimental type
is being created there. It's something to see these bearded, muscular "Lions of Judah" in the display of military might. It is
one thing to adjust to the sight of these hard-nosed men astride
horses or tractors or pulling in fishing nets, men for whom hard
work is almost a religion; but what is one to say of batallions of
unsmiling girls authoritatively toting machine guns? The self-
tortured, delicate-souled introspective Jew is unknown here, so
that creativity in the arts, if and when it comes, will probably
give rise to unusual forms.*

*The entire tone of the country is pragmatic and experimen-
tal, and perhaps in the kibbutz, as a self-contained, utterly
democratic community, a model is being hatched, worthy of
emulation. I could not help being reminded of our earlier
dreams about founding a private school in which there would
be a more intimate and organic relationship between study and
work and student and teacher—a relationship that would not
be severed by the ringing of a bell.*

KIBBUTZ AIYELET HASHAHAR
April 26, 1964

At Safad the hostel was full, and as I had only twenty
pounds left, and it was Thursday, which meant staying at a
hotel three nights, I decided to go to Kefar Hanasi and look for
Ennen Sonn.

No one there knew of her, but I was put up anyway, stayed
three nights and worked the last day at the fishpond. They
must have thought me a glum fellow, as I said not much to
anyone, and the English types did not induce me to overcome
my lack of sociability. I got a lift Sunday night to the ruins of
Hatzor, and, as a parting shot, the driver suggested I visit at
Ashahor just down the road. I did, and wandered into the stu-
dio of Mrs. Kuloth, who kindly took me to lunch, then for afternoon coffee and later fixed me up with a room. This place is

lovely, with beautiful trees and a pool. It does a brisk tourist business. Today I visited an English class—rather uninspired and unimaginative—and was struck by how essentially the same all students are. Later I hitchhiked to Hulota and Shmina and the wildlife sanctuary, which was jammed with busloads of noisy students.

This evening at the dining hall, I was invited to the home of another English teacher who was genuinely curious about my self-search, and told me how badly Israel needs "messengers" of my sort. She is still full of vision after thirty-three years of kibbutz life, and spoke of the great tasks that lie ahead in building a new culture, language and nation—and particularly of the problem of assimilating the new immigrants who come from nonwestern lands. These great challenges whet my appetite, but I told her that I thought myself a rather useless luxury, which this new state would neither need nor appreciate for a couple of generations to come. My openmindedness, my inclinations toward Christianity and my opinions of Jewish ritual as lacking any spiritual power, would probably disqualify me from citizenship and usefulness. She assured me this was not so. It was as obvious to her, as it is to me, that I was born for service. The only question is: "Where does my responsibility lie?"

HAIFA
May 3, 1964

I have just returned to my class "D" hotel after a melancholy stroll through the rather deserted streets of this lovely town. I started in the best of spirits, but something sad stole into my soul as I walked. Before long I was singing softly to myself from Franz Lehar, German love songs, and all the refrains of "Weltschmerz" that I know. I sense a German atmosphere here, or perhaps it is only that every bookstore is filled with German titles and handsome art books, portfolios and reproductions. What a hunger I have to paint!

The hour grew late, and rather than steep my melancholy with beer, I returned to the hotel and chatted briefly in Deutsch with the night-clerk who now is dozing near me in the lounge while I write.

What is it about things German that pierces me so deeply? Something forces the tears to press behind my eyes and makes my heart heavy. Tonight the sight of bookshops and art galleries next to furniture and houseware stores made me bite my lips and almost sob. Perhaps they are symbols of my Olympian and mundane needs, perhaps never to be reconciled or fulfilled—needs which the Germanic soul of a Goethe, Nietzsche or Hesse knew so well. Bittersweet pain convulses me again tonight, and I think especially of Helga and want to say, "Niemand liebt dich so viel wie ich" (No one loves you as much as I).

I think that what is best and deepest in that German feeling is the sense that life is delightful, dear and terribly sad—the residue that is left after the frenzy and fury are done with, the haunting and irrevocable "truth" that inheres in the nature of things, life's incompleteness and transiency; all overwhelm me. I could smash things this night or be very tender. Oh, where are Betty and Saul and all my loved ones when I need them most?

Part of my maudlin mood has been brought on by two long, painfully written letters from Inger—in their innocence, more powerfully evocative than any art. She is more rare than she can ever realize, and surely the finest, most selfless, honest and courageous soul I know. I have never been made to see more clearly the vanity of my corrupt heart. Never have I felt more wretched and despicable. The idea of putting the child up for adoption is utterly inconceivable to her, just as she will not permit me to breathe a word about abortion. This child is her life—her anchor in the world. Only I am floating free.

Betty's poetic and philosophical letter asks if faith does not have to meet the challenge of doubt. My days and nights are filled with just that struggle. I do not know who the real Art Katz is—only that he is both rotten and divine at the core. Betty chides me for my lack of discretion, yet I feel that discretion is like patriotism, a last refuge for scoundrels. Though it may on occasion be a virtue, I prefer to take the risk rather than to regret what was lost in safety.

Tonight I was particularly impressed by these words from *The Varieties of Religious Experience* by William James:

"Give up the feeling of responsibility, let go your hold, resign the care of your destiny to higher powers, be genuinely indifferent as to what becomes of it all, and you will find not only . . . inward relief, but often also, in addition, the particular goods you sincerely thought you were renouncing. This is the salvation through self-despair, the dying to be truly born. . . . To get to it, a critical point must usually be passed, a corner turned within one. Something must give way, a native hardness must break down and liquefy . . . Some say that the capacity or incapacity for it is what divides the religious from the merely moralistic character. . . . those who undergo it in its fullness . . . know; for they have actually felt the higher powers, in giving up the tension of their personal will. . . . the everlasting arms receive us if we confide absolutely in them, and give up the hereditary habit of relying on our personal strength, with its precautions that cannot shelter and safeguards that never save. . . . It is but giving your little private self a rest, and finding that a greater Self is there."

I have a portentous, almost fateful foreboding about the future. The very air I breathe crackles with a still unknown expectation. There is beyond all doubt a Force, or forces, at work on my life from sources outside my own creation. This, coupled with the knowledge that my mother will soon be arriving in Israel where I shall have my first face-to-face confrontation in many months, leaves me with a nagging tension, an incongruous combination of hope and despair.

LETTER TO MOTHER
HAIFA
May 8, 1964

Thanks for the check. I lost no time and sent Inger two hundred and fifty dollars which I suspect she can really use. The dear, courageous girl has taken herself a small apartment in Copenhagen to avoid causing her parents the pain that comes of small-town gossip. Her doctor has forced her to stop work, as her legs had become inflamed and swollen—but her expenses continue. I suspect another reason for moving was to spare me embarrassment, because she writes that I am "more delicate and vulnerable" than she, and "that she can better hold out from people's scandal and wickedness than I." You must read these long (ten to eleven pages) painfully written letters, and you will come to marvel as I do at the complete unselfishness of this simple and noble girl. She prays to God that I be given peace, and thinks only of my happiness and my feelings. I've come to realize through her how vain and self-centered I am and have always been. Even now I am thinking only of my convenience and future. What are my "gifts" and my strivings alongside the fine and noble character of this simple unlettered girl? What an "education" I have—and am yet to receive—at the cost of her pain. Yet, were it not so, I would likely have been doomed to be a vainglorious fool all my life. As it is, I still think I am rather hopeless and not man enough to change.

She writes: "I will not my family shall talk about you and me some human judge so hard they think not on what they say. I will not have you and my conditions dirt to that is for me so bright and clean. My family here in Copenhagen ask me about you and me. I not will tell them about you. They let me go

*along and in peace . . . Arthur, I think sometimes you think I
am unhappy because I shall have baby. I am not but very
happy for that. But that is so hard to live alone and so be pregnant.*"

I asked her if her parents know that I am Jewish, and what is
their reaction to that. She sputters angrily and accuses me of an
inferiority complex for even mentioning it and adds: "*A Jew is
also human as we are. Here in Denmark are all people equal
. . . and I am very happy and proud because you are a Jew,
and I know many human will envy me and baby.*"

To allay any fear you may have that I will remain in Denmark and waste away my "gifts and talents," I quote her
again: "*Remember you, what I say to you. I will not be a block
on your legs and I say that it is better for baby to live alone
with me, that it is not good for him to have parents as unhappy. That is better for him you come every year and so are
we all happy . . . You know if this miracle should come to pass
will I go to end of the world together with you. You know I will
not married of sympathy.*"

I'm looking forward to your arrival on the *Shalom*, and will
make plans to meet you at the dock.

KIBBUTZ YODEPHET
CENTRAL GALILEE
May 11, 1964

Strangely enough, at this kibbutz, founded by those seeking
a more truly spiritual life inbred with love, I received my
coldest reception. How can I ever forget my first meal here, on
a Sabbath, which I ate in stony silence, totally ignored. Nor
were subsequent meals any different. Although I sat alongside
the secretary, he made no attempt at an introduction or to
bring me into the conversation. When I later suggested to
Sarah, my new friend, that he might have done so, she replied
that it would have struck everyone as unnatural and forced.

"Natural" life really seems to be the keynote here, as I have never seen such slovenliness, unplanned and late meals, eating from the common bowl, gross table manners and loud and frequent "griping."

The Sabbath meal was not opened in any special manner, although it was by far the best meal in my four days here, and the only one with meat. I was told that it is usually followed by singing, although that did not take place on that night. Sarah told me that in the beginning there were special practices and observances, like, for example, a time set aside for silent meditation. But one by one they were all dropped, once everyone was caught up in the actual work of this young, going kibbutz.

Individuals did treat me well, especially Eton, the diesel mechanic, who was the first to greet me after my tiring trudge of six and a half kilometers up here. He talked to me and showed me about. The next afternoon I worked with Jo-ash on the grafted trees, and he, too, was very pleasant, informative and cordial. Aside from Eton and Sarah, no one showed the slightest curiosity about me or my purpose in being here. Understandably, they resent those who come for a look-see, having had sour experiences with previous Americans. The work was very hard for me—blisters formed quickly and my fingers cramped cutting weeds. The second day's work, lifting soggy fifty-pound bales of hay to dry, was no picnic either.

This afternoon I took a walk and picked peas with Sarah, who looks a bit like a hardened Ingrid Bergman. She's had a number of casual relationships and an abortion two months ago. When I asked how she could sleep with a man for whom she had no special feeling, she shrugged her head and said she didn't know.

I have learned that the kibbutz is in real danger of forgetting the purpose for which it was formed, and is getting entirely caught up in its workaday activities. They tell me the spiritual character will come of itself later, spontaneously, but I really doubt it. I think it must be planned and structured into the

daily life or it is lost. Perhaps it is too late already. What they
need is a spiritual leader along with the secretary, who, in this
case, is occupied solely with problems of an organic nature.

Personally, I found that I am not cut out to be a farmer. It
may be romantic in one's imagination, but trudging in mud or
dung, the smell, the flies, the burrows and thorns, getting
drenched in sudden downpours, simply does not appeal to me.
I really had my chance to see this by comparing my mild interest with Jo-ash's intense absorption when he spoke to me about
trees and grafting. At night I dreamed about being a muralist,
traveling from kibbutz to kibbutz, beautifying Israel. I could
smell the paint and feel the pleasures of the brush and the joy
in the executed work. This is far more my cup of tea.

Tomorrow I return to Jerusalem to spend a few more days
with Ben at the Hebrew University before meeting mother on
the maiden voyage of the *Shalom*. That same portentous feeling hangs over me tonight like a dense fog. I sense the over-
powering presence of God—

> *O Lord, thou hast searched me and known me.*
> *Thou knowest my downsitting and mine uprising,*
> *thou understandest my thought afar off.*
> *Thou compassest my path and my lying down,*
> *and art acquainted with all my ways.*
> *For there is not a word in my tongue, but, lo,*
> *O Lord, thou knowest it altogether.*
> *Thou has beset me behind and before,*
> *and laid thine hand upon me.*
> *Such knowledge is too wonderful for me;*
> *it is high, I cannot attain unto it.*
> *Whither shall I go from thy spirit?*
> *Or whither shall I flee from thy presence?*
> *If I ascend up into heaven, thou art there:*
> *If I make my bed in hell, behold, thou art there.*
> *If I take the wings of the morning, and*

dwell in the uttermost parts of the sea;
Even there shall thy hand lead me,
And thy right hand shall hold me . . .
For thou hast possessed my reins:
Thou hast covered me in my mother's womb.
I will praise thee; for I am fearfully and
        wonderfully made:
Marvellous are thy works; and that my soul
        knoweth right well . . .
Search me, O God, and know my heart:
Try me, and know my thoughts . . . and lead
        me in the way everlasting.

                                        (Psalm 139)

CHAPTER EIGHTEEN

I fled Him, down the nights and down the days;
I fled Him, down the arches of the years;
I fled Him, down the labyrinthine ways
    Of my own mind; and in the midst of tears
I hid from Him, and under running laughter.
    Up vistaed hopes I sped;
    And shot, precipitated,
Adown titanic glooms of chasmèd fears,
From these strong Feet that followed, followed after.
    But with unhurrying chase,
    And unperturbèd pace,
Deliberate speed, majestic instancy,
    They beat—and a Voice beat
    More instant than the Feet—
"All things betray thee, who betrayest Me."

Naked I wait Thy love's uplifted stroke!
My harness piece by piece Thou hast hewn from me,
    And smitten me to my knee;
    I am defenseless utterly.
    I slept, methinks, and woke,
And, slowly gazing, find me stripped in sleep . . .
                                    —Francis Thompson
                                    The Hound of Heaven

MESSIANIC ASSEMBLY
JERUSALEM
May 22, 1964

The events of the last few days are almost too incredible to record in this journal. Sometimes I hardly believe them myself.

After I spent several days with Ben at the Hebrew University, he arranged for me to visit a Hasidic community in order to observe the ultra-orthodox, the pious ones, in their daily habitat. Here, he felt, I would see Judaism in its finest flower and greatest historic expression. I agreed to go, eager to know the best that Judaism had to offer.

Thursday, yesterday, I took the bus from the Hebrew University. I'd ridden the bus many times before, but for some unexplainable reason I boarded the wrong one. I soon became aware that I was being driven through a portion of the city that was totally unfamiliar to me. After riding a short time, trying to orient myself, I realized I was hopelessly lost and got off the bus to seek directions.

I walked into a small bookshop, the first store I saw, and asked the woman behind the counter for directions. She answered me in English, and told me where to catch the bus that would take me back into familiar territory. As I turned to leave, I glanced at the books on the shelves. Bibles! Commentaries! Books with crosses on the covers! Christian literature! I was astounded, and turned and stared at the obviously Jewish-looking woman behind the counter. "What is this place?" I blurted out.

Her face was creased with smiles as she answered, "We're a congregation of Hebrew Christians." Something inside me stirred, then snapped. It was the same feeling I'd had when reading the New Testament on the Ionian Sea. "This is our bookstore adjoining the chapel," she continued.

I knew! I knew with a certitude that I was not to leave. At last, here was a place where I could find my answers! As if a dam had burst, I turned to her, pouring out my questions.

I didn't know there was such a thing as a Hebrew Christian. I thought I was the only Jew in the world who had ever been seriously attracted to Christ. But here I have found a group of Jewish believers, and have been told there are many, many others across the world who have gone through similar searching experiences and have come to the realization that Jesus is the Christ, our true Messiah.

I spent last night here, sleeping on a pew in the little chapel. This dear woman, Rena, has spent hours of her time answering my questions, and some of the others, along with her, have spent equal time praying with me and for me. I forgot all about visiting the Hasidic Community.

Jung speaks of the psychiatrist who cannot minister to his patients because they sense his feeling of disgust for the moral condition revealed in their confessions. This has not been so in my relationship with Rena. She has listened to my confessions. She has smelled the foul odors of the deep cesspools of my life as I have stirred and agitated the rotten crust. And she has never flinched. Never condemned. She has accepted me as I am and loved me. Never have I felt such acceptance . . . such unconditional love . . . such understanding.

Now, on the eve of my second night with them, we have just finished a long involved conversation around the meager supper table. I explained that I am not really Jewish in the religious sense, but rather Jewish in the existential sense. I have a growth of concerns, deep Jewish concerns, as evidenced in the modern Jewish writers, in a search for meaning and identity. What am I? Who am I? What does it mean to be Jewish? I feel I am a man out of place—in my generation and in the world. I feel I am designed for a world of real justice and brotherhood, but have not been able to comprehend nor realize its fulfillment in this institutional world of schools, marriages and synagogues.

Not only have I been quizzing these strange people, but I have argued with them. I know during that first reading of the New Testament more than four months ago that God poured

out upon me a revelation of His truth. I was made, then, to understand that there is a living God and that Jesus Christ is His
Son. But I have an aversion to becoming a conventional Christian. It is repugnant to my life and insulting to my intellect.
Now Rena tells me that there is a world of difference between
institutional, traditional, gentile Christianity and the life of the
"completed Jew," the spiritually born-again believer. It has
been very difficult for me to comprehend this. I am very much
confused and shall spend the night again occupying a pew in
the little chapel, reading until my eyes close from the little paperback volume of St. Augustine's *Confessions*.

> "Still bound to earth, I refused, O God, to fight on thy side
> as much afraid to be freed from all bonds, as I ought to have
> feared being trammeled by them.
> "Thus the thoughts by which I meditated upon thee were
> like the efforts of one who would awake, but being overpow-
> ered with sleepiness is soon asleep again. 'Awake, thou sleeper!'
> 'Presently, yes presently; wait a little while.' But the 'presently'
> had no present and the 'little while' grew long. For I was afraid
> thou wouldst hear me too soon and heal me of my disease of
> lust which I wished to satiate rather than to see extinguished
> . . . And I made another effort, and almost succeeded, yet I
> did not reach it, and did not grasp it, hesitating to die to death,
> and live to life; and the evil to which I was so wonted held me
> more than the better life I had not tried."
>
> Confessions of St. Augustine

MESSIANIC ASSEMBLY
JERUSALEM
May 24, 1964
LETTER TO GOD

*Dear God: I wish I could say that this attempt to communi-
cate with you was occasioned by a spirit groaning under the
weight of its iniquity and for whom prayer was an inadequate*

outlet. You know me too well for that. You have led me here to this community of believers and given me counsel and learning with a saintly woman. You have given me all the solitude and opportunity needed to find my way to You; and yet I fail to find it. I admit that I am more aware of Your holy presence than ever before and readily acknowledge the Bible as Your Word. Still, it is a faith that is partial and not quite genuine. You have made me realize that the total faith You require is something that I cannot achieve by myself, and I pray for Your help. My nature and all that I have labored to create in all the years that I have been at the center of my life is not to be surrendered that easily. Yet I do yearn to be born again to live the more abundant life in You. Your Holy Book tells me that I may know You only through Your Only begotten Son who was sacrificed on the Cross for the remission of my sins and that I need only believe in Him to be saved, to be made whole.

I believe. Help my unbelief! I think to myself that I am prepared to die to this life—to give up everything to be reborn again to serve You—to be blessed that I might be a blessing to others. Yet I have not the strength to part with my love of self, my sensuality, lust, gluttony and extreme delight in the pleasures of this world, though if You were fully real to me I would not hesitate. My nature will not yield up its incredulity and is reluctant to part with accustomed ways though I am weary of this half-life. I yearn for Your joy. You are beckoning me to take on this deeper reality, to consecrate my life to Your holy purpose, and I am not man enough to accept so great a gift.

My flirtation with You is a sometime thing and my prayers pitifully weak and fitful. You say, "ask and it will be given," so I ask You once more to help me to perceive You as the living reality and to transform each tainted word from my mouth so that it will be genuine and heartfelt. Make me fully to understand the full meaning of my sin so that I shrink from my natural man and willingly yield him up; let me die to this world so I can be born again. Let me enter the Kingdom of God as a

*child. Give me that faith and power of belief. And God, forgive
me the sins which I here confess to You:*

VANITY: *I have constantly sought my own glorification at
the expense of others and ostensibly for "noble and just" ends
—that I might be glorified.*

LUST: *There is a constant lecher in my heart and I needn't
tell You the tragic consequences of the present moment nor of
the recent past—which I know I would repeat again if the opportunity provided itself.*

PRIDE: *Perhaps the worst offense of all, Lord, for it sepa-
rates me from You and makes me exult in my puny gifts and
accomplishments, stature and appearance so that I defer to this
world rather than to Your call.*

GLUTTONY: *I can't even put aside a cigarette for You and
am constantly eating to excess.*

INDOLENCE: *I'm indifferent, lazy and choose to do only
that which is self-pleasing.*

IRRESPONSIBILITY: *I assume responsibility only to the
point of convenience unless otherwise prodded.*

RESENTMENT: *I am beginning to sense many resentments
toward people, resentments that border on hatred toward anyone who threatens my ego. I confess resentment even toward
You for allowing me to be instructed in Your Word by a
woman, Rena.*

*There are many more I could list, Jesus—INSINCERITY,
SELF-DECEPTION, COWARDICE, and EGOCENTRISM.
But You know them all far better than I.*

Am I ready to die to
The flattery and applause of others?
My sense of self-esteem?
Delight in my physical appearance?
My so-called reason and intellect?
My desire for comfort and creature gratification? Help me,

*Oh God, I ask only of You—for You alone have the answer for
me.*

MESSIANIC ASSEMBLY
May 25, 1964 (5:15 a.m.)

Sister Rena interrupted my "letter to God" last night, talking with me in her lovely intense and devout way about the
problem of my salvation. After acknowledging that God cannot be forced, she granted that I was quite right: what was
needed was for God to make more real to me His own reality,
the significance of Jesus' sacrifice and the depth and depravity
of my own nature and sins. All of these were for me shallow
and cerebral understandings only, on top of which I was
afflicted with a peculiar indifference and sudden spiritual de-
cline which affects me still at this writing. Rena made the most
beautiful prayer over me, "reminding" Jesus that He has said if
two or three gather in His name He will be there also. Then
she asked that I be flooded with His Holy Spirit and that
through a dream or some other way I be led to genuine repen-
tance and conversion. Although she obviously expressed God's
will, I once again (I had been prayed for by a group the very
first night and then by Lars, a Danish fellow, the following
day.) was left completely untouched.

I must confess that even in the moment of her prayer I had
an involuntary flirting desire about her which although rela-
tively "innocent" was certainly incompatible with the purity
of the moment. I think I would touch her, or have her touch
me, that I might tap that wonderful spiritual force that constantly courses in her. Yet I fear that in the touch my desires of
the flesh would form a sufficient dam to block the flow of
power.

I know in my heart that I am far from truly realizing myself
as a sinner, let alone repenting to the point of abhorring myself—dust and ashes for Job. I am not ready gladly to sacrifice

this worthless husk to God and cry out to Jesus to enter my heart as my personal Messiah. Nor am I ready to truly believe on His name. I am certainly a long way from being "reborn." I do believe that "he who asketh receiveth," but I know in my heart that I am not really asking. It is only my lips that move.

Furthermore, "not everyone that saith unto me, Lord, Lord, shall enter into the Kingdom of Heaven, but he that doeth the will of my father which is in Heaven." I know that I am *very* far from that. So first, Rena tells me, I must *obey*. Then *ask*, *fully desiring* what I ask for. Then I must *believe* that God keeps His promises, and that what I ask for is in fact *granted*. "Whatsoever things ye desire, when ye pray, believe that ye have received them and ye shall have them." To rid myself of the final carnality that binds me to this world I must surrender, unconditionally, my will, my desires, my very self—the corrupt and self-defeating center of my life.

I have tried to sacrifice my happiness and desires while kneeling at the old altar in the chapel, all to no avail. My appetites, always insatiable, cannot be slashed. It is self (ego) that is at the crux; *it* is the "indwelling sin" (the seat of that incorrigible bias toward sin). Rena tells me that only Jesus' blood can wash it out. Would that I could bring myself to really believe that! That would be the hope for all mankind for it "cleanses out of the heart all hatred, envy, malice, bitterness, temper and pride." If roots of bitterness were washed away, all that is contrary to love purified, then love could blossom out to perfection, and the fruit of the Spirit—love, joy, peace, long-suffering (patience in love), gentleness, goodness (love in action), faith, meekness (love stooping), and temperance (love controlling) could be made manifest.

It is only through the moment by moment power of the life of Jesus that we can love God and our neighbor, Rena tells me. "We are all as an unclean thing, and all our deeds of righteousness are as dirty rags." (Isaiah 64:6) In short, LOVE, as I've

long contended, *is* at the center of the Universe, the means to
which I now know—if I am man enough to seek it.

It means upsetting and putting in reverse order the self and
all the tendencies that for a lifetime have been natural to it.
Here is the crux of man's freedom, wherein he can take the
first faltering step toward God and break the deadening deter-
ministic chain wherein he is trapped. This way surpasses
human genius and ingenuity. It is sublime and irrevocable
proof of God's being. In a stroke, the way is provided whereby
man can find the way to himself, his fellowman, and God—all
organically, symbolically, and mysteriously related one to another. The schism between obligation to God, to one's fellowman and to one's self which has long caused me anguish could
be ended for *all time*. But I am still not man enough to receive
Him.

MESSIANIC ASSEMBLY
May 25, 1964 (11:00 p.m.)

Tonight is my fourth night in this place. Rena, Lars and others have labored hard with me and have diligently encircled
me with prayer. But so far there has been no breakthrough,
and I am beginning to wonder if there will ever be. It seems almost impossible for me to grasp the account of the Old Testament and its prophecies of the coming of the Messiah, God's
plan for salvation, the concept of sin, and many other things.
My intellect, which I realize is a barrier to faith, refuses to
bend and accept these aspects of God's revelation. I know I
have been brought to this crossroad, and I know that what I
have heard here is true. But so far the pieces have not been
put together.

After supper Rena and Lars sat with me around the table.
Both had their Bibles before them and we discussed the term
which had always been anathema to Jews—CONVERSION.
"Conversion: turning from one position or direction to an-

other; passing from one side to another." So says Webster. Lars says for him it meant stopping and turning.

Rena says the idea of "turning" is basic. She quoted several Old Testament passages along this line. One I remember came from II Chronicles: "If my people, which are called by my name, shall humble themselves, and pray, and seek my face, and turn from their wicked ways; then will I hear from Heaven, and will forgive their sin, and will heal their land."

"Conversion, Arthur," she said, "is the voluntary change in the mind of a sinner in which he turns *from* sin *to* Jesus Christ, and from being a god unto himself to the Living God."

My argumentative nature flared forth. And even though I have been confessing my "sins" privately, I am still not accustomed to having others refer to me as a "sinner." "Why do you call me a sinner. I'm as good . . ."

It was Lars who interrupted in a gentle way saying, "Sin, Art, is wanting to have your own way rather than surrendering yourself to God's way. By this definition, are you a sinner?"

I had already confessed too much to back him down. I retreated from argument while Rena flipped through the Old Testament reading verse after verse to prove God's eternal plan was for man to repent and be converted. "A new heart also will I give you and a new spirit will I put in you; and I will give you a new heart of flesh."

She went ahead to explain this passage from the prophet Ezekiel by saying, "God is the creator of the new heart and the new spirit, but it still remains for you to take that step in the 'new direction.' " She then quoted another Ezekiel passage, "Cast away from you all your transgressions, whereby ye have transgressed; and make a new heart and new spirit: for why will ye die, O house of Israel?"

They both spent a long time trying to reason with me. "Art, no one can be converted except with the consent of his own free will. God will not override human choice. He has been at work in your life all these years to bring you to this one point.

Now it is up to you. We may not be free to choose because sin has dominion over our lives, but we are free to refuse. You can refuse to be chosen."

Everything that Rena said made sense but there was still some kind of block.

They prayed around me before we left the table, after which I returned to the little chapel and turned again to St. Augustine, spending some time reading from his own deep experience of conversion.

"I flung myself down under a fig tree and gave free course to my tears. I sent up these sorrowful cries: 'How long, how long? Tomorrow and tomorrow? Why not now? Why not this very hour make an end to my uncleanness?'

"I was saying these things and weeping in the most bitter contrition of my heart, when suddenly I heard the voice of a boy or a girl—I know not which—coming from the neighboring house, chanting over and over again, 'Take and read, take and read, take and read.' Immediately I ceased weeping and began to ask whether it was usual for children in some kind of game to sing such a song, for I could not remember ever having heard the like.

"I got to my feet, since I could not but think that this was a divine command to open the Bible and read the first passage I should light upon. I quickly returned to the bench where Alypius was sitting, for there I had put down the apostle's book when I had left. I snatched it up, opened it, and in silence read the passage on which my eyes first fell:'let us conduct ourselves becomingly, as in the day; not in reveling and drunkenness, not in debauchery and licentiousness, not in quarreling and jealousy. But put on the Lord Jesus Christ, and make no provision for the flesh, to gratify its desires.'

"I wanted to read no further, nor did I need to. For instantly, as the sentence ended, there was infused in my heart some-

thing like the light of full certainty, and all the gloom of doubt
vanished away."

The Confessions of St. Augustine

How I wished it were so for me!

Vivid in my memory tonight is an incident that took place when I was seventeen. I was hitchhiking from Los Angeles to New York, learning to drive as I traveled by telling the men who picked me up that I knew how. We were somewhere outside of Cleveland, and I was at the wheel, the owner of the car asleep in the seat beside me. The highpowered automobile responded beautifully to my touch as I pushed the accelerator to the floor and fairly flew down the highway. I overtook a much slower car on a hill and swerved to pass. Just at that instant another car came over the crest of the hill, heading directly toward me. I slammed on the brakes with every ounce of muscle and nerve! I could see the other driver doing the same thing. In a split second, as we careened toward each other, I saw the look on his face—pain, anguish, stark terror—as our two cars, shaking and quaking, tried to stop the enormous momentum we had developed. In that frantic split second I felt all of life slammed into reverse as the brakes finally grabbed, and we screeched past each other, missing one another by only a fraction of an inch.

This is the way I feel tonight. I'm on a collision course. I'm being challenged—just as Abram my ancestor was challenged —to leave nation, kindred, and father's house and walk into an unknown land of total separation. I'm being called by some unknown force to leave all that is familiar and dear and walk into a foolishness and absurdity which promises nothing but a cross. I feel the mighty foot of an Unknown God slamming on the brakes of my life—yet the thrust of my thirty-five years plus the accumulated momentum of centuries of Jewish tradition, makes it almost impossible for me to change direction. But I cannot escape the words of Jesus: "Except ye be *con-*

verted, and become as little children, ye shall not enter into the Kingdom of Heaven."

I've seen my mother, on several occasions, when confronted with the God of Jesus Christ, go livid with rage and begin to shake and quake. Is this a typical Jewish reaction? Confront us with man—confront us with progress—confront us with the concepts of justice—confront us with humanism—but never, never confront us with the God of Jesus Christ. Why? Why should I react this way? Tonight I sense that whether I come from a background of traditional Judaism or blatant atheism, it makes no difference, for all is vanity. To become a Christian is impossible. In my mind this is synonymous with becoming a Gentile and embracing all that is repulsive to me. Yet even though I cannot understand it, I realize that until I am brought to the point of seeing God as presented in Jesus Christ, all is lost. For here, and here alone, is reality.

My eyes are tired now and my hand shakes from so much tension. I think the answer will never come, and I am ready to give up. I shall write down this last passage from William James's *Varieties of Religious Experience* and then stretch out on this hard pew to try to sleep.

"So long as any secular safeguard is clung to, so long is the surrender incomplete, the vital crisis is not passed, fear still stands sentinel and mistrust of the Divine obtains . . . Fling yourself upon God's providence without making any reserve whatsoever . . . only when the sacrifice is ruthless and reckless will the higher safety really arrive."

MESSIANIC ASSEMBLY
May 26, 1964

"It was deep calling unto deep, the deep that my own strug gle had opened up within being answered by the unfathomable deep without."

—*William James*

In my sleep it came. Last night I was agitated out of my skull, not being able to put together the things that Rena was trying to tell me. But in my sleep last night it came together. It was not a dream exactly. It was simply an understanding, given by the Spirit of God who has been leading me all these fourteen months. I saw the pattern that He had been following. None of these episodes and encounters have been by chance. He has plotted and masterminded every move. Last night I saw it. It was like a great painting, with God standing in front of the easel laying His brush to the canvas of my life and stroke by stroke bringing me into being. As the image developed I could see God returning again and again to the palette, blending colors with swirls and strokes, dabbing hard here and stroking gently there, until I saw myself painted against the backdrop of eternity—and saw God revealed in Jesus Christ.

It has all been God. It was He who allowed me to become a Marxist. It was He who allowed me to attend that Institute. It was He who allowed me to try my hand at vocations, lusts, and every human device to find resolution—all to bring me to this particular juncture, this crossroad! It was He who took me by the hand, and, as a father would lead a child, led me step by step into this new spiritual understanding which now permeates my very soul. But now He says: "I can take you no further. It is up to you to receive or reject this Jesus as your Messiah."

Thus as I awoke this morning with the sound of stirrings in the next room, I lay with my head cradled in my arms, looking up at the ceiling, feeling the hardness of the wooden pew against my back, saying with silent lips, "I now take you as my Saviour and Lord."

Strange, since my life has always been such a tumultuous cauldron of emotion, that what has happened to me has been so calm. Here, in the most telling and significant moment of my life, I actually *feel* nothing. I simply accept what I now *know* to be true, and this morning there is a tremendous peace and calm in my life—peace that actually passes all understanding.

This morning at breakfast I turned to Rena. "Rena, I believe." She slowly lowered her cup of coffee to the saucer and looked at me.

"What do you believe, Arthur?" I groped for words and stuttered as I answered, "It's not *what* I believe, it's in *whom* I believe. Last night He came to me—the Risen Christ—and He touched my mind and unsnarled all the tangles of doubt. I believe in Him and have accepted Him as my Master."

She looked deep into my eyes. Then her own eyes filled with tears and she began to shout: "THANK YOU, GOD! HALLELUJAH!" She leaped to her feet, knocking over her chair and spilling the coffee on the table. Falling on her knees she lifted both hands over her head, and with tears running down, and an expression of angelic exuberance on her face, she praised God. "Thank you, Lord, for answering my prayer of last night when I prayed, 'Lord, make this stubborn man to understand.'"

I was slightly confused, not knowing whether to join her on the floor, whether to raise my hands and shout, or exactly what to do. I stayed in my chair and watched her. There was enough happiness in her worship for both of us. However, I was feeling a strange quietness and peace settling over my life. My anxieties over Inger, my guilt over Helga, my resentment over mother—all seemed to be washed away in this new found relationship with the Messiah.

Rena rejoined me, taking her seat at the table. After reminding me of Moses, the epitome of the modern man of his day, who lost his status and wandered in the wilderness before encountering God at Mt. Horeb, she led me in this prayer which I now record as a statement of my commitment.

"O GOD OF MY FATHERS—ABRAHAM, ISAAC AND JACOB. THE GOD OF MY OWN SAVIOUR, JESHUA. I HAND MYSELF OVER TO YOU NOW. I SURRENDER *ALL*. TAKE ME AS I AM AND MAKE ME WHAT I OUGHT TO BE, FOR THE SAKE OF THY GLORY ALONE. SO HELP ME GOD."

Arthur Katz

CHAPTER NINETEEN

Only three days have elapsed since my mother's arrival in Israel and my flight here to Vienna. It is a time fraught with implications and consequences which I sense more than understand. Yet it is profoundly important that I do understand. I saw in that short encounter with my mother all the "signs" of worldliness which I must prepare either to accept or disavow.

I met her in Haifa as the *Shalom* pulled into dock. The moment they lowered the gangplank I heard her voice over the din and noise of the crowd. Nothing had changed from the old days—her glazed-eyed, nervous features, her confusion, her shrill grating voice—all indicated that she was the same as ever. I was very disappointed.

She had made a mistake in her choice of a traveling partner and did not know how to extricate herself. The other woman, a constant nag, was always in the way, an encumbrance. How typical of my mother to make her own bed of thorns.

Five minutes into our first chat I realized sadly that any hope of real communication was futile. The experience at Jerusalem, concluded only the day before, was very alive in me—and yet it was precisely in the spiritual matter that I succeeded least in communicating. What a contrast to my talks with Rena! The two women seem the epitomes of two ultimately opposed value systems. Rena emphasized my absolute obligations to God and His righteousness, and my mother stressed my responsibility for my own (and hers, indirectly) self-glory and gratification. I sense for the first time a clash of systems, with my mother the embodiment of the spirit of this world— the practicality—the "Yiddisha Koph."

The issue, of course, was Inger. Whereas Rena had indicated that I was going to have to consider marriage as an honorable path to follow, my mother's greatest fear was that I would marry her. I tried to explain to her that I had no intention of marrying Inger, but was simply promising to be with her when the baby was born. She fears, however, that if I return to Denmark my heart will somehow be touched enough for me to do something rash and submit myself to a life of obscurity, rotting away in Denmark, buried in the domestic round, and neglect, ultimately losing, my gifts, which *she* has bestowed on me, and whatever future they promised.

I was very impressed with Rena's analogy of Moses. Born as a prince and destined for large things in Egypt, he nevertheless had to "waste" forty years in obscurity as a shepherd before assuming the task God gave him. Furthermore, those years were a preparation without which the task could not have been undertaken. Rena suggested that God may intend for Denmark to be my "desert" even though it would seem a turning away from God's work, my teaching in California. She suggested that perhaps God intends my gifts for "evangelism," mentioning that Paul spent three years in Asia before assuming his apostleship. My vanity was flattered, though I know these gifts are not my own but were given me to be consecrated in God's service.

Underlying all this is the nagging confusion concerning Helga. I know that my relationship with her shall never be ended. Divorce actually settles nothing. It is simply the public admission of failure. The problem still remains, and now that I am under orders from God, I find that Jesus has some rather pointed things to say about divorce and remarriage. I am caught on the horns of a terrible dilemma and my mother's nearly hysterical utterances are not helpful.

I realized during our first conversation that I could not last out the whole week in the company of mother and her friends. So I used Vienna as an excuse to escape a few days earlier and still arrive in Denmark on June 1, as planned. In my mother's chatter I realized the bankruptcy of self-striving which never satisfies and only leaves one more desperately empty at the end. I felt pity for this woman who had learned so little and who now was crying for me to provide meaning for her life. I could see how much we really have in common, yet her dynamism, physical attractiveness, and power of personality have been fretted away in a senseless fury. The same fate will surely befall me if I take the wrong turn now. Only God can lead me to safety.

These few days spent in Vienna have been pleasant, though the city itself has not the splendor of joyfulness I expected. Two outings to the Wienerwald (Vienna Woods), where I spent a good bit of time attempting to heal up the wounds of mother's visit and gain some strength for what lies ahead, were good for me. And Boden and Krevzingen castles have been delightful. Rushing last evening from Boden to the Volkoper to hear *Die Lustige Witwe* (*The Merry Widow*), I jumped aboard a train, sweating and breathless, and found myself face to face with a tall, elegant, lovely girl who smiled and answered my questions about directions graciously. She turned and said, "Auf Wiedersehen," when she left the tram, and I was pierced through by her loveliness and the hunger it awakened. The opera and its hauntingly sweet arias only added to my melancholy, and I was suddenly aware that my lust was still waiting for its opportunity. My experience with Christ was enough to give me a new direction, a new desire in life. But I still need something more to enable me to overcome temptation and give me power to live for Him.

I did have an encounter with an American boy at the youth hostel who was deeply disturbed and anxious about his life despite his exterior calm and glibness. With him I found myself sharing the Gospel, and he confessed to me his fears about his sexual and homosexual experiences. What need a man fear about his sexuality, I asked, if it evolved unhurriedly in love rather than in spasmodic and illicit furtive episodes? Failure wouldn't be so personally and psychically catastrophic if a man's vanity were not the center of his life. We spent the day together, walking in the woods, and I gave some account of my own spiritual journey and tried to suggest to him the solace, profundity, and application of the Gospels which he had come to disown as so many irrelevancies. I know that he accepted my words and that he had been brought to see that the idea of God is not antithetical to the modern, "sophisticated" mind. Once more I had confirmation through him that a man's life cannot be whole without God. However, he had not the courage to accept this on faith and scoffed at the idea that the sexual malady was but a symptom, as Jung suggests, of the deeper spiritual distress. He solidly disavowed any implication that his relationship with his mother could possibly be at the root of his sexual abnormalities and that only a redeeming, forgiving experience of grace could change this. Probably our talk did me more good than him, as it helped clarify my own convictions. It's interesting, however, that the first two people to whom I have tried to "witness"—my mother and John—have both misunderstood me and either laughed, scoffed, or ignored my testimony. I hope this is not an omen of things to come.

CHAPTER TWENTY

How my heart was touched as I flew over Denmark yesterday afternoon. It was so soothingly beautiful in its woods and
lush green and yellow patches. Inger's note was waiting for me
at the airport, and I took the bus to Randers where she had
been waiting many hours. She was looking better than I expected with her swollen stomach.

My first encounter with her family went off fairly well—all
things considered. As tired as I was, Inger and I stayed up most
of the night talking. Once again I was caught up in her strange
intenseness and authentic personality so difficult to describe to
others. For the first time I saw the lovely natural auburn of her
hair and complementary complexion—part of the prototype to
which I have always been the most responsive. I keep looking
at her, sensing in her the most pointed challenge of my life.
There is something about her that is deeper than deep. More
than ever I feel that this "episode" is more than mere happen-
stance. I cannot shake the feeling that in my response to it the
entire meaning of my life is at stake.

Concerning the problem of Inger's future: I see that I must
soon commit myself, for if she is to be settled in her apartment
in Copenhagen, I must help her. Being away from her parents
and tied down with a newborn infant will not be easy. I feel an
almost eerie presence with us in the room, as if God Himself is
overhearing everything and watching the way in which I will
decide. Selfish as usual, I find the idea of living in Copenhagen

attractive, where hopefully, I could paint, write, and pursue my studies in peace. Could that be God's intention also?

I am sitting now in this living room that is so unfamiliar, a bit of cosmic dust, oily and effusive to be sure, while the family life goes on undisturbed about me. Sitting opposite me, sewing, is this strange, uncluttered particle whose love for me is total and unconditional, sustaining matter-of-factly in that swollen stomach the uncommon conjoining of ancient and disparate bloods which is soon to become, to what end God only knows, a miraculous new fact in the universe. Strange, strange, strange that I should come to this inexplicable pass. What does it mean? Why? It cannot be that all this is an accident without meaning and purpose.

At the same time I am totally free. I can do as I please—walk out of here in five minutes and this girl will make no attempt to stay me. She asks for nothing, yet I am everything to her. I am at the critical juncture of my life. How I respond to it morally will make me more or less the man I will choose to be.

With a word I can postpone—who knows for how long?—my return to the states, my calling, the possible fulfillment of my "gifts," for a probable headlong rush into obscurity. Yet even as I ponder my decision I feel with certainty beyond explanation that all of the steps have already been taken for me and though I may deliberate wearily over each, it is inevitable that I must be led from one to the other through to the end. It is almost as if it were prepared before the foundation of my life.

The baby is due any moment, and I am so nearly broke I must obtain some kind of employment—hopefully the kind that will give me sufficient leisure to paint—the hunger for it grows daily—to write, study, and continue my quest and attempt to order my life in God's plan.

LETTER TO SAUL GOLDMAN
HAMMERSHOJ
June 3, 1964

*Dear Fellow: I would tell you everything if I understood it
myself and knew you wouldn't scoff, but it is all so strange and
odd that the words seem blunt and void of descriptive powers.*

*Tonight I am sitting in a Gentile home in a little community
of five hundred with all these Danes around me who speak not
a word of English. Looking at this homely girl with the monstrous stomach I think,* What am I doing here? How did I get
here? What does all this mean?

*I have a sense that men are not the masters of their fate, but
are pushed, manipulated by forces not only beyond our control
but beyond our comprehension.*

*Inger's mother is distressed. Not that her daughter is preg-
nant—that is quite normal for unmarried Danish girls—but
rather that she is pregnant by a foreigner. My mother is distressed that Inger is pregnant. Not that I have done anything
wrong, but that the fact of her pregnancy might deter my
course from the goals she has set for me.*

Thus you can get the picture.

*If I did not think of you as "ruthlessly" logical it would be
easier to write you of what I have been feeling of late. It is so
ambiguous, a weight beyond words, that I fear it will simply
not stand your keen scrutiny. So Saul, baby, for my sake relax
the cerebral center and let me touch you with my heart in hope
that we have not lost that common sense of reality and intimate contact that was once so important to me.*

*Dear chap, I am down, down, down, and I know that it is not
a fleeting mood but a deep knowledge that the world is indeed
a stale, flat, and profitless place. All my life has been a turning
up one street and then another, and though often wearied, I
had a sense of expectation always humming in my blood. Now
it is through. I have come to the last street, and know that they
are all the same and I am tired . . . tired of all that walking
and having only a dull ache inside for all my pains.*

What have the thirty-five years meant? What am I now? What possible significance can all this have on the future? Events seem to be propelling me rather than I them. What's worse, day by day this gristle, this actuality, seems less real. But then, looking back, were my years with Helga "real"? Was that silly, confused, misspent woman who visited me shortly before I left Israel actually my mother? Is this dear, patient, loving creature—she walks on tiptoes not to disturb me as I write—who carries my child in that immense, almost humorous stomach, possibly the one with whom I shall spend the rest of my life?

But most important and yet mystifying is a soul-shattering experience that took place in Jerusalem—an experience I almost hesitate to mention. I say, "hesitate," for at the moment it seems so far removed—and yet still so real. Be it what it was, something happened that has inalterably changed the mainstream of my life. It has been slow, but something is changing in me, like tastes turning over.

Yes, I find myself in the doldrums of doubt and despair, and even as I write, I have doubts whether to tell you "all." But we have searched for Truth so long together—long and tedious have been the hours that the two of us sat up seeking the elements of truth, wisdom and justice. We differed in that you were the theorist, the perfectionist, and I the existentialist. How natural that I should have found myself thrust heart first into this experience of reality—and now find myself quite unable to communicate any of my experience to you. All my theories of God, man, sin, salvation, past, present and future have been bombed away, exploded into dust, because of one perfect moment of peace and reality.

Perhaps, Saul, my desire to share will one day be fulfilled. There are still many unanswered questions—enough that I am holding off from a full explanation of this experience. But when the time comes I shall saturate your brain with my newfound discoveries of truth and attempt to satisfy your analytical inquisitiveness with what I know to be real.

*I set out a year ago hungry, seeking experiences in reality.
And I have found it (or has it found me?) but it sits on me like
a huge indigestible lump serving only to deaden my sensitivity
and make me thick and gross. What, my fellow? Have you a
tonic for me? Can you light some hope in me or are we both
afflicted by this world? Only God can reach out and sustain me
in this pass (I know what you think of that), but He is excruciatingly silent, unlike that group of Christians with whom I
spent those four days before leaving Jerusalem. (And with that
revelation I perhaps give you some insight into the new bent of
my life.)*

*You can see plainly how badly I need to hear from you.
When you see Helga, give her my dearest regards.*

COPENHAGEN
June 12, 1964

I just finished reading the paperback novel I bought today
while Inger visited at the hospital. It's by a San Francisco psy
choanalyst—about a search for meaning. It awoke terrible
poignancies in me and stirred me deeper in my soul-sickness so
that I am prompted to write this.

I slept this afternoon and had a bad dream in which Helga
was pregnant and somehow promised me the child. We were
to have a rendezvous and I recall my looking down from a
height and recognizing her emerging from a car and then
walking to what seemed to be a lakeshore. Suddenly her move-
ments became erratic and I was aware she had gone berserk.
When I raced down the incline to where she had been standing, she was gone, and a man told me she had been taken into
custody. The same man implied, in his tone and looks, that I
was responsible for her breakdown.

Inger told me I talked in my sleep and called to Helga. On
occasion great waves of remorse and pity overcome me when
I think of Helga and wonder how she is and what she is doing.

It pains me to think of the anguish I have caused her, and I will never forget the terrible tears rolling down her face when I took her to that home for Jewish women in San Francisco. I could then and now have run myself and the car into the brick wall when I saw that pain and my constricted but intractable heart. The imprint of our seven years together is deep in me, and I doubt if I will ever be able to—or want to—shake it loose.

The recollection of our house itself, the symbol of our last hope, brings me almost to tears. Often I am tempted to picture myself back in it, picking up the strands of life with Helga. I remember her delight in puttering about the house and cooking, baking and playing hostess. I was too self-centered ever to accord her the recognition and appreciation she deserved—which in its own way, I know, contributed mightily to her emotional and psychological downfall. I pray that God will comfort that wounded, often tortured, spirit.

Now this other dear bundle sleeps at my side as I write, bearing that absurd bulge I call her "football," which Helga yearned for and which might have saved our marriage. But I have not the wisdom to know whether it should be saved, or even to know in my own heart if there is love there or not. I feel so tenderly affectionate to my present "kitten"—did I call Helga that also? I feel I could almost make my life with both of them, but perhaps most rightly with Helga who has the longest investment although she was, and perhaps always will be, incapable of loving me as dear Inger does. My life is a mess—and each day I become more acutely aware of the crisis I am in and my incapability of resolving it. Can even God untangle such a life?

Today I feel homesick—but what or where is my home? Saul and Betty are like a home base for me, but have lives of their own, and our relationship may not be the same on my return. What then would be left for me there but to be a haunted, sickly creature burning in the flesh and capable as

ever of terrible indiscretions. Were there only some power—
beyond my salvation—in which the power of God Himself
could flow into me, giving me the power to rise above these situations which pull me down, down, down.

I'm contemplating writing a novel in which the hero attempts to reconstruct his marriage after a long separation, but
his good intentions bring misery and finally destruction to his
wife. So could it be with me should I attempt it. Then, what of
this baby that is to come? Inger is convinced that I will ultimately return to it and her after finding disappointment in
California, and perhaps she is right. Where and with whom
does God intend for me to find completion? I know my nature,
that I must find the door to myself through the love and understanding of another. Will it ever come?

COPENHAGEN
June 15, 1964 (11:00 a.m.)

I am tired and numb and have just returned from the hospital after seeing Inger and the baby. We have a boy with black
hair and my nose—not at all a pretty baby, but then only
about two hours old when I saw him. Just what Inger wanted.

The whole thing has happened so matter-of-factly that its
import has yet to reach me. I displayed none of the celebrated
stereotyped reactions of intense anxiety, nervousness, and then
joy but remained calm, even rather glum, upon seeing the
baby. Is it that I hear the bells toll?

Yesterday afternoon Inger and I visited her uncle and aunt
in Kastrup, had some company till about 10:00 p.m. and then
went to bed—or rather I read and Inger "patchkied." Soon she
felt some pains which continued to get worse though I thought
at first that they were her usual nightly pains and would eventually subside. I had come to accept her pregnancy as a "permanent" feature; the huge bulge, the pains—all were ends in
themselves—and I almost disbelieved that a baby was to come

from it. By 3:30 a.m. I was sure that it was the real thing, but she would not let me take her to the hospital earlier because she was told to expect eighteen to twenty-four hours of labor and wanted me with her as long as possible. The hospital does not permit the father to wait around. I left the hospital, expecting that the baby would not come till tonight or later, and was roused from my sleep by her cousin, Sonja, who had been telephoned that the baby came at 7:30 a.m., only two and a half hours after I left her. Even during the most intense pain before we left the apartment, Inger, typically considerate beyond words, was apologetic for disturbing my sleep and wanted to close herself in the kitchen so that I would not hear her moaning and crying. I thank God the whole thing has gone well.

Babies have always left me cold, but the couple last night brought their eight-month-old son—a beautiful baby who laughs, giggles, and is keenly aware of, though perplexed by, his surroundings—and I was amazed to see that already he had a distinct personality and was a real entity rather than some amorphous bundle. I thought to myself, *How can I afford to miss any stage in my own baby's development? And how can I deny my child my presence?*

I am a father now. Can it be? I can still scarcely believe it! I thought for a long time that I was one of those who were fated not to be fathers. In fact I did not share this hunger that most men have for a son, but thought this longing to affect posterity would come through creative achievement of my own.

But do we make our own lives? God has shown me my impotence and fallibility and rebuked me in the most ironic circumstances for my vain presumptions. This little, homely, simple Inger—who is to me less homely, more dear, and more lovely as the days flash by—whose love for me is vast and strange because it is completely unselfish and has nothing to do with my looks, character or accomplishments, has become, through a chain of the most odd, effortless and artless circumstances, the mother of my child. That seed which has been nurtured through generations of thousands of years of ancient God-covenanted people that began with Abraham has now given fruit through a relationship between a Jew and a Scandinavian. I take heart when I remember that David, yea Christ, came from a strain that began with a mixing of the nationalities between Boaz the Hebrew and Ruth the Moabitess. It is a miracle that I can scarcely believe, and what it portends for the future I do not even dare imagine. However else my life may be a failure, meaningless and unfulfilled, through me has been created a substance of living potentiality touched with some of the madness of my own nature—a son in whom life's meaning may be better realized than it has been in me. Perhaps that madness, tempered by sweet Inger's love and loyalty, may blossom into greatness undeveloped in either father or mother.

How often in the frenzy and seeming futility of her own life has my mother expressed that hope for me? This is mankind's perennial hope—one that renews our life and upholds us against despair and defeat—that one day my son, though he has just now made his entry into the world, will express *my* fondest dreams and frustrated hopes.

We have thought much about a name and have decided to call him David. I wanted a name that would remind him of his ancient ancestry, a Hebrew name, and Inger liked this best. I like the David of the Bible who was shepherd, poet, king—beloved of God and God-intoxicated, though all too human in his lust and covetousness. Beyond that, it does pay some small homage to another David, the father I never knew. God grant that I shall not prove as faithless to my son as my father was to me.

COPENHAGEN
June 17, 1964
LETTER TO RENA

*Dear Saintly Sister Rena: Your tender, solicitous letter was
received this morning and broke down my last resistance to
write you, which reluctance, I suppose, was based on my suspi-
cion that what I would have to say would be a disappointment.
I have, as you rightly suspect, fallen back "into the world"
since I left you. I have glanced at my Bible in only the most
cursory fashion, and my prayers have been brief even in the
face of my deepest depression, when I feel life and the world to
be purposeless and meaningless. For a while I even doubted my
own sense of reality, feeling that events were propelling me
rather than I them. It was as if control of this life had slipped
from my hands. Is this how the "Holy Spirit" of which you
spoke works? In becoming a Christian does one actually ac-
quiesce to the Spirit of God—surrender all control to Him?*

*On the encouragement side of the ledger, even though I have
been unable to maintain the spiritual intensity I achieved
through you, I have not returned to what I was before, and
there is every evidence that something deep within my life has
actually been changed—as you would say, "converted."*

*The trauma that I expected and needed to shake me and
bring me closer to God did not come with the birth of the baby.
So I hang as suspended as ever, still lacking the fullness of the
realization of my turning to Christ which I so badly need. I am
convinced more than ever that He is the way and the truth, but
so far it seems to be only a cerebral awareness and not a commitment of my total being.*

*In William James' chapter on "Conversion" he speaks of the
volitional type, as opposed to those whose psychic makeup is
more prone to self-surrender, in whom the regenerative change
is usually gradual and consists in the building up, piece by
piece, of a new set of moral and spiritual habits. So perhaps
there is still hope for me, though I must go about it in my*

characteristically plodding way through study and contemplation rather than have it as a dramatic mystical experience. In this way I am arming myself with a knowledge that will be very valuable in countering objections to God in dialogues with so-called "modern" men, of whose ranks I so recently was, and still bear the traces. So perhaps it is God's wisdom after all to lead me through this "wilderness of the mind."

I wonder if you still recognize me in all this, or do I express a tone, a taint, of the world not to your liking?

I have confided in you in all frankness and hope I have not distressed you too deeply. I feel strongly attached to you, for you are more to me than God's vehicle. I appreciate your concern, and want and need your counsel, hoping fervently that you do not give me up as a "lost cause." By the way—confessions of a scoundrel and rogue—I have resumed smoking—as much or more than ever. What else am I to do if I am not to sit like a lump when I am in a room full of curious people, looking me over and talking around me because I cannot speak their language? Besides, Denmark is very creature-comfort-oriented with good beer, cigars, and tobacco, and one can hardly resist the temptation. Through all this pleasure, though, and with their progressive civilization to boot, I sense at the bottom a lack of real joy and can almost hear their collective sighs and groanings at this life.

June 18, 1964

What can I say of the last two weeks? More and more I draw into myself and fall silent despite the cordial reception of Inger's family and every effort on the part of Inger, herself, to make me happy. In a sense I am cut off from normal intercourse, because I cannot speak their language, but I know that even if I could, I have no inclination for conversation. Only my homely and simple Inger sustains me in my despondency, and she grows more dear, more authentic each day. Her nature is deep and her character strong. She is tireless and uncomplain-

ing, and there is no question but that she will make a devoted
mother. She is quite prepared for me to leave her again—even
this moment if my happiness requires it—and tells me that one
moment with me sustains her for a year.

I am still uncertain whether to return to California or not. I
am anxious to go for many reasons but primarily because I cannot gauge what effect this year away has had on me until I
view myself again from the old setting, i.e., in front of my students. Furthermore, my strong feeling of duty to my students
aside, I have come to realize the value they serve in drawing
me out of myself, making me constantly plumb my own
depths, understand and order my own thoughts in lively inter-
change with them. I have been a passive spectator this past
year—a sponge absorbing experiences, and now my nature
prods me to give. The fact that I am not doing so accounts in
large part for my moroseness.

On the other hand I cannot escape this sense of responsibility I feel toward Inger and the baby. Marriage would be honorable but preposterous. My relationship with Helga was far
more compatible than this could ever be. We can't even speak
the same language. I can promise her nothing except some
small financial assistance for the child; yet she does not even
ask for this. What should I do? No, that is not the question!
Rather, what does God want in all this? Yet how does He
speak? And how do I listen?

LETTER FROM SAUL GOLDMAN
June 19, 1964

*Since I finished reading your recent letter I have felt a gnaw-
ing obligation to answer promptly, but frankly I don't know
what I can say without sounding foolish. Your letter seems to
cry out for advice—or solace—but I don't really think you
want either, and I am fairly certain that my spiritual power is
not strong enough to help you overcome your depression. I am*

prefacing my letter in this way because I know that I am going to say some foolish things and I want to have a disclaimer going for me in the first paragraph.

You mention that God is excruciatingly silent. If I may slip for a moment into the character of a religious figure (I am a Universal man, don't forget), let me say—and this is something of a cliché, I suppose—that if it seems to a man that God is silent, perhaps the man himself is at fault. I am not joking. Perhaps the real significance of your quest is that your actions have led you to the point where life seems to have no significance.

Let me talk about myself. I am anything but happy. I go to the office in the morning and I come home rather fatigued in the evening. I often ask myself, "How long am I going to go on like this?" Then I consider the possibility of returning to teaching. Never! It is beneath my dignity—I mean it—to associate with jackasses. Please understand that I am still in my character as a religious figure. A jackass, if you like, is an unreligious person—a person who doesn't give enough of a damn about life to live it with zest, to strive with his own God given resources to come to terms with the human mystery. I read the letter you recently sent to Betty. In it you mention staring at Inger's stomach and wondering what it's all about. Well, I want to tell you that I think that's really fine—there's hope for you yet.

Now what is it that I wanted to say? Something like this: What has happened to you can be explained romantically or it can be explained in the most matter-of-fact way ("Katz slept with a Shiksa in Denmark"), but the reality is somewhere between the extremes of possible explanation. Life is both spiritual and matter-of-fact at the same time. What could be more obvious? I know for certain that this is true. I know that I don't have to be a schoolteacher to be spiritual, or to be part of the world of ideas—I only have to have that kind of consciousness of the human mystery that you have right now.

To take another approach, I'm beginning to think that there's hope for a serious individual in his thirties, if he can be ruth-

lessly honest about his own experience. I believe that in previous years I was a victim of many false myths. I have become immune to them. I now accept the sheer horror that lies beneath the surface of things, and I go out of my way to avoid encountering that horror so frequently that I become distressed with my methods of escapism from the realities of life. My life is so empty and void of meaning, and if you have found some answer, any answer, to satisfy this spiritual hunger then I want to hear of it. I suspect that you have found some kind of reality in Christ. (Am I getting close?) I shudder at the possibility of this, but if there is an answer to man's misery, emptiness and shallowness in this approach then I am willing to open my mind objectively to any truth you may have discovered.

Is all this talk getting us anywhere? I think we need a long face-to-face conversation. Are we going to have one soon? Are you coming back to teach at Inglewood? I suspect that if you do, you will find it rather dull going. Maybe you ought to stay in Denmark for a few months. Don't forget that you have money in the Retirement Fund. I realize that you are going to have a tough time making a decision, but make one and stick to it. What else can a man do?

I think that there are still all kinds of possibilities for my future, but to take advantage of them I will have to change my mind. And on that cryptic note I leave you.

COPENHAGEN
June 18, 1964

Yesterday I ran into Lars, the Dane I had met at the Messianic Assembly in Jerusalem. Strange that I should see him the same day I wrote Rena. We renewed old acquaintances and I spoke to him about my doubts and spiritual powerlessness. Lars reminded me that I had entered into a "covenant" relationship with God, much as Abraham had entered such a relationship. All I have to do, he said, is claim the promise. God has taken the covenant seriously whether I do or not.

Lars said, "There is more to Christianity than the mere acknowledgment of Jesus as Saviour. Beyond salvation is the possibility of receiving the very power of God into our minds and bodies through the process of being filled with God's Spirit."

I immediately recognized that familiar expression used by Rena. Lars continued, his entire countenance energized with power as we drank coffee at a small open café. "This is brought to pass by yielding your spirit to the Spirit of God. The victorious Christian life cannot be lived in your own power, Art. Inner stability in the midst of an unstable world comes only through the power of God's Spirit in the very essence of your being."

I understood little of what he said but could not deny the authority with which he spoke. Nor could I deny the evidence of his own personal experience attested by his fervent witness.

Lars invited me to attend a service with him at a Pentecostal Church last night. It was all very strange. I enjoyed the spirit of the place even though I didn't understand a word of the service. Lars whispered to me some of the things that were taking place, but mostly I sat musing to myself. I was Art Katz the natural man—but at the same time Art Katz to whom something had happened. I knew I had a foot in two worlds— spiritual and natural—and was unhappy in both. Unfitted for both.

I was talking to myself. "When will I really break through this and understand?" And I heard a voice—an audible voice —that said, "Be patient. It will come."

I looked around, but no one else seemed to have heard it. Lars was intent on the sermon, which was in Danish. I said to myself, "Well, Katz, now it's happened. You're really psyching yourself out. The strain has been too much and now you're hearing voices."

But the voice was real, too real to dismiss as a mere psychological phenomenon. It was the voice of God—telling me that one day He would complete the work in my life. My question is, can I last that long?

July 20, 1964

Something was born in my heart this evening. I had been disturbed all afternoon by the intimations of some friends that Inger had had many boyfriends, was impulsive of heart, that if it were not me it would be someone else, and that she could easily marry another man after I left.

I said to myself, "Oh no, Inger too? Have I been deceived again? Has she lied to me or played with me by keeping things from me?" Old wounds were reopened, and Inger, seeing my pained expression, soon had me confess all these doubts to her. She looked me straight in the eye and said that she had never lied to me nor kept anything from me. Merely one half-look at her was enough for me to know that I should never have doubted.

Seeing her with the baby pressed to her bosom, his tiny head tucked beneath her chin, her downward glances of beaming love, pride, and care gave me the impression that she had been a mother forever. My wound was healed and something new— something akin to the reflections I had only in dreams—a sense of love for God, for her, for the baby—a love that fills, satisfies and overflows—crept into my heart in its stead.

As with my convenant relationship with God, can it be that I have also entered into some mysterious covenant relationship with Inger? Must I, rather than struggling to comprehend, merely relax and claim that which has been promised? I sense that I am about to be led out of this wilderness, by a pillar of cloud by day and a pillar of fire by night. What lies ahead remains unknown, but for the first time, even though my way still seems blocked by the giants of Anak, I catch the wafting scent of milk and honey.

> *"And the Lord spake unto me saying,*
> *Ye have compassed this mountain*
> *long enough: Turn you northward."*
>
> Deuteronomy 2:2–3

CHAPTER TWENTY-ONE

OAKLAND, CALIFORNIA
May 5, 1967

It's been almost three years since my last entry. I had not intended to write again, but the poignant events of this afternoon have so stimulated my heart that I am driven to sort through the maze of jumbled school papers on my desk to find the journal and make this report.

I've just returned from Saul's funeral. The service was quiet and dignified. I can still feel the firmness of Inger's hand in mine as we followed the small group of mourners out of the little chapel. The soft afternoon sunlight streaming through the open door into the semidarkness of the church gave us the impression of emerging from the dark tunnel of pain and suffering into the magnificent light of eternity.

Saul's death, coming as it did so suddenly, has greatly shaken me. He had been a believer only a short time. I knew he was seriously considering the claims of Christ on his life, but was still overwhelmed that day when he called me weeping, telling of a revelation he had received in his living room.

The last conversation we had was six months ago. He was preparing to leave for Europe on a study grant, and we had played tennis that morning and then returned here where Inger fixed us breakfast. Afterward we sat around the table talking. I still didn't know the depth of his Christian experience, whether he'd just had a flirtation with Christ or whether he'd entered into a covenant relationship.

Later he wrote me from England about Sandy, the girl he planned to marry as soon as he returned from Europe.

The next thing I knew he was dead. He and Sandy had left Washington to spend their honeymoon driving back across the states. In Nevada they stopped at a motel. Sandy had been teaching Saul how to swim and left him resting beside the pool while she returned to the room. When she went back to join him, she discovered him floating face down, having struck his head in a fall.

Today I was deeply touched by the display of strength and courage shown by Saul's bride of only a week. She was a paragon of peace and calmness.

"Art, I know Saul was a believer," she told me this afternoon. "He read his Bible every night on our honeymoon. The night before he died he said, 'I don't understand how any Jew can refuse Jesus as Messiah, after reading the Prophets and the New Testament.'"

Saul was the one friend who didn't turn his back when I told him of my experience with Christ. He alone listened intently to my long dissertations and asked probing questions about my experience. How different from Marty and Betty. Betty flew into a fit of such uncontrollable rage when I tried to share my testimony with her that I had to get out of her car at a stoplight and walk the rest of the way home. How different from the reaction of Sid Zimmerman who gave me my first New Testament and whose last letter still lies on my desk: "Look Art, I must tell you that you should not waste breath on my recruitment. Although I'm happy you have achieved happiness, I don't find it pleasant to have it trumpeted in my direction. I simply refuse to accept a concept of God which is able to be written down, preached, or believed in. To box God into one form called Christ is insufficient in my eyes . . ."

Dear Saul. How my heart is wrenched now to think that I could have spent time with you praying in the Spirit—discussing the deeper things of God. I think of all those vain hours we spent in idle chatter. Ah, old friend, how good it would have been to have spent the time delving into the things of eternity. Now that privilege is yours to experience—and mine to await.

I was made particularly aware of how much of my life I had spent in idle chatter the first night after my return to California. A woman who had been my colleague in teaching invited my old friends for a party. I sat there strangely quiet, feeling no compulsion to speak. His new peace was upon me. My so-called intellectual friends were engaged in one of their snorting discussions. The fur was really flying, but I was completely out of it. At midnight someone turned to me and said, "Art, what's with you? You've been strangely silent all evening. It's not like you. You're usually in the thick of these discussions."

"I'm sorry," I said, "but I just find this conversation completely irrelevant to life."

That was a strange thing for me to say because I had never before seen the truth of it. God had just made me conscious of how we intellectuals exult in talk for its own sake. How profitless it really is.

"Just what do you think is relevant?" my hostess asked me then. I had to pause because just the night before, arriving in California on the bus, I'd said, "Lord, I'm going to keep my mouth shut because this is yet too soon for me to speak, and I don't want to botch it for you."

But when she asked the question, I felt an impending challenge. I knew I must go on and give my first testimony. I prayed under my breath, "Now, Lord, give me words to speak." All talk stopped, and everyone turned to face me. They had all known me as a leading radical on that high school faculty. I began to speak of how God had led me to Himself. I explained that I was a fundamental believer, that I believed in the entire word of God and had received Jesus as my Messiah. Their jaws dropped. We had a conversation that night until three or four in the morning. God led me to see how shallow was their profession of being real radicals and how vain and empty and posturing the parading and carrying of signs and

distributing of placards and leaflets is. I saw clearly where th
true revolution really is.

These people, who almost without exception were seein
psychiatrists, betraying one another, involved in deceit an
treachery, were telling me that I had "flipped" and that I, wh
was now enjoying the peace of God, should see a psychiatrist

David just opened the door to my study and after shyl
peeking in, bounded across the room to his favorite place o
my knee. His excuse was an untied shoelace. I've tousled hi
hair, and now he's gone, no doubt to play with his baby sister
He's left the door ajar and I catch the aroma of Inger's matzo
ball soup as she prepares dinner. What a wonderful respit
after the tensions and demands of the week past.

Yesterday I received a notice to stop by the principal'
office. He'd had complaints from parents who objected to m
using the classroom to witness to God, to suggest that in Hi
"Way" was the solution to all life's entangled problems.

Still weighing heavily on my heart is a confrontation at Mar
vin Roth's cocktail party two years ago. There in his beautifu
home overlooking the bay I met one of my former students a
Inglewood, now a bushy-headed radical at the University. I re
membered him as an intense young man who once thought o
entering the Presbyterian ministry. I had negated his ideas, rid
iculed his faith, scorned him for his naïveté. That night a
Roth's, glass in hand, he told me, "You were right, Katz. Jesu
is a fascist."

Strange that my atheistic philosophies did not bring scathin
complaints from parents as my Christian witness seems to do
But now I'm given the choice of resigning or—

Shall I leave? Perhaps this is God's way of directing me int
that other ministry. I have been invited to participate in a
outreach to my own people. Perhaps . . . At this point I an
unsure. There is so much happening at once.

This afternoon after the service Inger and I were standin
on the front walk of the chapel when I saw Helga come out o
the building. I stood stunned for a moment, looking at he

ghostlike figure and face drained of life and energy. She was thin, stooped, and her eyes were sunk deep in her head. I had seen her only once since my return from Europe. I pointed her out to Inger, who immediately began tugging me toward her. Helga was now standing on the sidewalk, smoking a cigarette and staring blankly at the hearse that was pulling away from the curb.

Inger put her arm naturally around Helga's waist and said simply, "I'm Inger." Helga looked at us curiously, as if she were trying to remember. She nodded her head and said, "I'm glad to meet you." Glancing back at me she asked, "How are you, Art?" Her voice came from another country.

Inger invited Helga to come home with us for dinner, but Helga's eyes showed no trace of emotion—or understanding. "That would be nice," she said. And crushing her cigarette on the sidewalk, she stepped off the curb into the cab that had just arrived. I had the weird feeling that she never really recognized us—

Tomorrow Britt will be in San Francisco. She called last week from Los Angeles where she is visiting friends and asked me to meet her at the bus station. I vacillated and told her to call me when she got to town. For two days I let my thoughts run with unbridled fervor. But last night, as we sat around the table after supper, reading from the Bible and thanking God for His mercy and love, I knew that I could never go back. Later in the evening, as Inger and I walked around the block, I told her of my temptation and decision. She said nothing, only clasped my arm with both her hands, looked up at me with her sparkling eyes, crinkled her nose and squeezed a little harder.

Bless the Lord, O my soul . . . who forgiveth all thine iniquities . . . who redeemeth thy life from destruction . . . who satisfieth thy mouth with good things.

After we had put the children to bed, Inger and I lay in bed together. I was silent, peering upward into the darkness, conscious of Inger's gentle breathing beside me. I let my mind wander through the gallery of portraits of the past . . . faces of those I have touched and hurt, yes, nearly destroyed. I moved from one portrait to another, pausing to remember and grieve. They start with Mother, then Helga, Rachel, Britt . . . on and on they go. The list seems endless. Some, like Rachel, are gone. She died soon after I returned from Europe. Some, like Mother, are still the center of my prayers. If only she could know the depth of my new love for her in Christ.

But Inger is ever beside me. I felt the warmth of her body and soft touch of her hand as she instinctively sensed the torment of my mind. Turning toward me, she nuzzled her face against my neck, whispering softly, "I love you, my Arthur— and so does Jesus." And in this simple utterance from this simple girl I find the answers to all my questions, the fulfillment of all my desires, the end of all my searching.

Fear not: for I have redeemed thee,
I have called thee by thy name; thou art mine.
When thou passest through the waters, I will be with thee;
And through the rivers, they shall not overflow thee:
When thou walkest through the fire, thou shalt not be burned
Neither shall the flame kindle upon thee.
For I am the Lord thy God,
The Holy One of Israel,
Thy Saviour.

—Isaiah 43:1–3

CHAPTER TWENTY-TWO

Kansas City
March 6, 1970

Another three years have gone by and I make this final entry. There have been so many changes . . .

When I prayed to know God's will in my relationship with Inger I was careful to stipulate that if it pleased Him to bring her to California to marry me, He would have to give me a loving disposition toward her. Otherwise, eventually it would simply be a repetition of the same mistakes I had made with Helga. I was fearful of devouring Inger with my temper or consuming her with my desire to dominate. I realized it would have to be God who made this marriage—although I thought such a thing was clearly impossible.

I learned that with God nothing is impossible. My prayer has been answered above all I could ask or think. God has done a great work in Inger also. Inger, who always slept with a light on . . . Inger, who twice attempted suicide in her adolescent years . . . Inger, who lived on a battery of pills. That same Inger—but no, He makes all things new. The new Inger, the Inger with whom God has satisfied my longing for a soulmate, now patiently bears the long absences on my part, maintains our home, manages our three children, and is mother hen, confidante and loving evangelist to the constant stream of people who come to her luncheons, her coffees and even stay to live with us while God straightens their disordered lives.

The greatest testimony my mother ever received was from Inger one night in Brooklyn. The two of them were seated together on a couch, my mother wringing her hands and ruing the spiritual awakening of her son, and lamenting "My boy, my boy!"

Inger turned to her and said, "But, Mom, I had to accept Jesus also."

Mother looked surprised. "What do you mean, you had to accept Jesus also? You were born a Christian."

"No," Inger shook her head gently and smiled, "I was born a Lutheran. *But I became a believer.*"

My mother's face mirrored the dawning of a new understanding. That was three years ago and even though mother is not yet a professed believer, she shows signs of softening and mellowing. On my last trip to New York I stayed overnight with her. She still protested when I tried to witness to her, but allowed me to continue speaking. When I told her that Jesus was being crucified at the same time the lambs were being slain for the Passover, she was startled and cried out across the table to her husband, "Is that true?"

I have the decided impression that my words are hitting home—partly because of the changes mother sees in my life.

These changes became more evident as I moved deeper into my experience with God. Yet the full measure of love, compassion, patience, power and strength which the New Testament promised were still not complete in me..

"Art," my friends explained, "this experience you are seeking is the very same the first Jewish believers received on the day of Pentecost or Shovuos as spoken by the prophet Joel in the Hebrew Scriptures: 'And it shall come to pass in the last days, saith God, I will pour out of my spirit upon all flesh: and your sons and your daughters shall prophesy, and your young men shall see visions, and your old men shall dream dreams; and on my servants and on my handmaidens I will pour out in those days of my Spirit; and they shall prophesy.' "

I submitted to their ministry and was prayed over many times. Nothing happened. I began to believe that I was some kind of spiritual leper, an intellectual somehow unfit to receive this blessing from God. Yet as I sought, I became increasingly aware of the deep problems still in me. God seemed to be gradually bringing all this to my attention.

Then one night in northern California, at the home of the Fultz family, I asked my hostess why she, a Gentile, had such an intense love for Jews. The Fultzes were studying Hebrew and making plans to go to Israel. They had a great knowledge of Jewish culture and a love for prophecy.

"I don't know," she answered, "but I do know that our God loves the children of Israel, and I love them also."

When it came time to go home we all stood up. Someone in the group said to the host, "Bob, you pray aloud and if anyone feels inclined to follow, let them do so."

I wasn't prepared to pray aloud. I was still a self-conscious, reticent man, not given to public displays. Bob commenced praying. When he finished there was silence. I sensed a strange Presence in the room. No one made a move to leave.

I kept my place, knowing that I was in the midst of people much deeper in the things of God. Bob prayed again. One by one the others followed, this time praying in a language I had never heard. My awareness of God was deep—intense. I fell to my knees and as I closed my eyes I felt the tears squeezing from under the lids. Then, in a torrential downpour, I began to weep. I imagined myself in some ancient synagogue, the people wailing in Hebrew.

Suddenly I felt the gentle touch of hands upon my head.

One of the group, an Israeli girl, had gotten up from her chair and walked to where I now knelt. Standing behind me she became a human channel for the Spirit of God. I felt the breath of God and tasted of His glory. I knew God was revealing only a minute portion of Himself, had it been anything greater I would not have been able to survive. I would have died. In that unspeakably beautiful moment I was suddenly aware my hands were above my head as I heard myself praising God without restraint. All elements of inhibition and self-consciousness were removed and oblivious to all surroundings I moved into His courts of Praise. It was a face to face encounter with the glory of God. I felt bands bursting around my chest and heart . . . I was gasping, sucking air as if I had never before really breathed. It was a moment of exhilarating freedom as I felt burdens and constraints snapping, popping and letting loose.

My spirit, long walled with the accumulation and residue of congealed anger, resentment, hostility and bitterness was suddenly set free. These residual stones that made up this wall had formed over the years. My mind had forgotten them, but they had taken up residence around my heart, forming a partition between myself and other men—and the Heart of God. The times I had been deeply wounded, the times I had been betrayed by those I trusted, the times I had been sinned against —all had coalesced and become a veritable prison.

In that same moment, I felt myself passing through a dark chasm, a tunnel of death. Freed from the bondage of self-will I felt my roots, for so long wrapped tightly around the stone blocks of self-defeating egotism begin to be nurtured by wellsprings of living water. The forces which had driven me to seek love and meaning through exploitation, arrogance and pride were flushed from my spirit and suddenly I felt impeccaoly and immaculately clean. In that split second of complete selflessness I felt the Spirit of God surging in as the waters of the Red Sea must have rushed together after the children of Israel had marched through to freedom. I stood in the Holy of Holies, praising God with total freedom as the ancient names of Yahweh and Jehovah took on a new meaning. From deep within me I began to magnify the God of Israel in a mystical language of praise as I rejoiced at the fulfilling of Jesus' prophecy for my life: "out of his heart shall flow rivers of living water."

I now realized what had happened to me six years ago in Jerusalem.

This redemptive power of God transforming my human personality had in an instant, by His Spirit, cleansed and worked in my heart, in the deep crevices, the dark places where men could not penetrate. The enormity of our human crises cannot be met with the inadequacies of our human solutions and conventional wisdom. How often even is our "spiritual" counsel hardly more than an inept humanism couched in the jargon of religion.

Religious teachers using such terms as "God as you understand Him," "God as an impersonal force in the universe" give us nothing to fill the inner void of our understanding. Rabbis rejoicing that we've come such a long way from the "archaic" and "primitive" notions of an "anthropomorphic" God who can actually see the iniquities and infirmities of men fail to show us even the shadowy substance of the real God who hears the cries of His people and stretches forth His hand to save.

This is knowing God in Spirit and Truth: not turning Jews away from their heritage but more fully and deeply experiencing it. Jewish believers have not deserted their faith. They have come to the heart and depth of it. Having come to the fulfillment of Messianic Judaism they are now all the more the Jew—true Jews fulfilled in Christ.

As those early Jews who were followers of the living Christ gathered together and prayed, "grant unto thy servants that with all boldness they may speak thy word by stretching forth thine hand to heal: and that signs and wonders may be done by the name of the Holy Child Jesus," so are we seeing the hand of the Lord work such miracles even now.

When Jesus was asked by John's disciples, "Art thou he that should come? Or look we for another?" Jesus answered, "Go your way, and tell John what things ye have seen and heard—how the blind see, the lame walk, the lepers are cleansed, the deaf hear, the dead are raised, to the poor the gospel is preached. And blessed is he, whosoever shall not be offended in me."

So it must be with this Son of Israel who now unashamedly claims the totality of the promise of the New Covenant, "for as many as believed, to them gave he the power to become the Sons of God."

"Behold, the days come, saith the Lord, that I will make a new covenant with the house of Israel, and with the house of Judah:

Not according to the covenant that I made with their fathers in the day that I took them by the hand to bring them out of the land of Egypt; which my covenant they brake, although I was an husband unto them, saith the Lord:

But this shall be the covenant that I will make with the house of Israel; After those days, saith the Lord, I will put my law in their inward parts, and write it in their hearts; and will be their God, and they shall be my people.

And they shall teach no more every man his neighbour, and every man his brother, saying, Know the Lord: for they shall

all know me, from the least of them unto the greatest of them, saith the Lord: for I will forgive their iniquity, and I will remember their sin no more."

Jeremiah 31:31–34

Publisher's Note:

Comments, inquiries, and requests for speaking engagements should be directed to:

Arthur Katz
Box 613
Plainfield, New Jersey 07060
U.S.A.

Write today for your sample copies of

⊕**LOGOS**JOURNAL

North America's largest charismatic magazine

and

NATIONAL COURIER

the exciting new tabloid

accurately reporting and commenting on news

of the world with a Christian perspective

Name _____

Address _____

City _____ State _____ Zip _____

☐ Send me a sample copy of *Logos Journal*
☐ Send me a sample copy of the *National Courier*

*(Please enclose 50 cents per sample for
handling and shipping)*